Sunday Snowdowns with **60 MINUTES**

Sunday Showdowns with **60 MINUTES**

15 years of dueling America's most feared TV news magazine—and winning!

Ken Fairchild

arena publishing
Dallas, Texas

© 1998 by Ken Fairchild

All rights reserved. No part of this publication may be reproduced, stored in a retrieval system, or transmitted, in any form or by any means, electronic, mechanical, photocopying, recording, or otherwise, without the prior written permission of the publisher.

This book is available at substantial quantity discounts to companies, educational institutions and professional organizations. For information, write:

Arena Publishing Co.
Business Book Division
Box 174
Preston Forest Center
Dallas, Texas, 75230-2718

ISBN: 1-57502-902-2

Printed in the USA by

MORRIS PUBLISHING

3212 East Highway 30 • Kearney, NE 68847 • 1-800-650-7888

To Don Hewitt, Mike, Morley, Ed, Leslie, Dan, Diane, Meredith, Steve and, of course, Harry, who have made our lives so exciting; to Jack Hilton, Steve May and Jack Williams who invented our profession; to those rare executives willing to face the cameras; and most of all, to those brave corporate communications professionals who truly put their jobs on the line by even suggesting it; this book is respectfully dedicated.

Acknowledgements

I need to thank my partner Pete Oppel whose name doesn't appear in these pages as much as it probably should because he has dealt with *Prime Time Live*, *Dateline* and other programs more than *60 Minutes*. He, being a newspaper veteran, also played a major role in the final editing of this book.

Lisa LeMaster's name does appear a lot, but not nearly enough to really reflect what she has meant to the profession and to my life.

Thanks to Lynn Fairchild, my brother, who labored many hours over a computer to make my words look something like a book.

And special thanks to the clients, way to numerous to mention, who have urged for all these years that this book be written, and who have shared my excitement that it is really happening.

Ken Fairchild
Dallas, Texas

Table of Contents

Foreword xi

Chapter One
Trouble Brewing 1

Chapter Two
Soul Searching and Ambush Journalism 19

Chapter Three
A Time Bomb on Every Corner 29

Chapter Four
Saying No 39

Chapter Five
Fighting Back 49

Chapter Six
The Stars 61

Chapter Seven
The Producers and Their Dirty Tricks 73

Chapter Eight
The Blues 83

Chapter Nine
Blues Two 95

Chapter Ten
The Clones 111

Chapter Eleven
Friend of Bill 123

Chapter Twelve
Should I, or Shouldn't I? 137

Chapter Thirteen
A Strategy for Winning 147

Appendix 155

Index 157

Foreword

It's usually at the top of any "You know it's going to be a bad day when ..." list. "You know it's going to be a bad day when your secretary calls and says a crew from *60 Minutes* is in the lobby."

For a quarter of a century, those words and corollaries such as "Mike Wallace is here to see you," or "Isn't that Ed Bradley down there on the parking lot with that TV camera?" have struck terror into the hearts of America's toughest corporate executives. Men and women who would face (and have faced) hostile takeovers, union boycotts, and even international terrorism, are ready to climb into the harness of their golden parachutes and seek early retirement rather than face the dreaded *60 Minutes* cameras, homing in tightly on perspiring brow and quivering lip while one of those self-assured, smiling, even soft spoken interviewers asks personal questions they wouldn't expect their mother's to ask them in the privacy of their own homes.

And for more than half of those 25 years, my partners and I have made a living helping those executives survive, and even win, those confrontations. After fighting more than a score of those battles, twenty-five at the time of this writing to be precise, we feel qualified to ask, "Who's afraid of *60 Minutes*?"

We've been asked many times over the years, "Why would any businessman or woman agree to go on *60 Minutes*? Don't they know the results can only be bad? Don't they know they will only come out looking ridiculous, or worse?"

My short answer usually is that I believe if *60 Minutes* is going to do a story on your company, it probably will turn out better if you participate. No one can tell your story better. One alternative is that the "other side"—competitors, disgruntled former employees, activists of one stripe or another, regulators— *someone* will tell your story. Another possibility, and one doesn't preclude the other, is that Mike Wallace or Ed Bradley will stand outside your office, pointing up at your window or at a closed door, and pronounce those fateful words:

"And up there in the ivory tower, Mr. or Ms. Business Executive refused to talk to us."

"But," the person who raised the question about why anyone would do it usually responds, "no matter what you say, they'll edit it to make it come out the way they want it to. You can't win."

This is simply not true, and, as you will see in these pages, we have example after example to prove it. With *60 Minutes*, as with any media exposure, there are dangers and pitfalls that can destroy those who are unprepared, or arrogant, or who simply have no honest story to tell. Yes, there are times when a company should say "no" to *60 Minutes*, and we will devote a chapter to how and why that decision might be made and the best ways to say "no." But, *if* you have a story to tell, and *if* you are properly prepared to tell it, you have you have nothing to fear from *60 Minutes*.

Chapter One

Trouble Brewing

Our first direct confrontation with *60 Minutes* came in 1982. Mike Wallace personally called a Coors executive, John McCarty, to tell him the CBS news magazine was interested in doing a story about what had already become a longstanding union boycott of Coors. Ordinarily that call would come from a producer or an associate producer, not from one of the "stars." Wallace made the call himself because he and McCarty had once been in school together. Maybe that acquaintance affected McCarty's decision and maybe not, but he did what few executives did, even in the early '80s. He considered the advantages to Coors of cooperating with *60 Minutes*, and with the help of Shirley Richard, who headed Coors' corporate communications, and John Meadows, head of community relations, McCarty convinced Joe and Bill

Chapter One

Coors, the brothers who ran the privately owned brewery in Golden, Colorado, to do just that.

Shirley Richard and John Meadows seemed to welcome the challenge like General George Patton looked forward to meeting Irwin Rommel in their classic tank battle in North Africa, and they planned their campaign accordingly. They reexamined every aspect of the union boycott, analyzing Coors' strengths and weaknesses, compiling documentation to support the positive arguments or to refute the negatives. They began a continuing dialogue with the *60 Minutes* staff about what CBS would be expecting, who would be interviewed on all sides of the story, what some of the key issues might be that they would want Coors spokespersons to address. They called Fairchild/LeMaster in Dallas and asked for our help.

With J. Walter Thompson and later with my own company in New York, then with the new media consulting company Lisa LeMaster and I formed in Dallas in 1980, I had been involved for several years in training Coors executives to deal with the media. We had worked with Joe and Bill and with their sons, Pete and Jeff, who were moving into active management of the company. Coors knew the value of good media relations. The media had helped create what had come to be known as "the Coors mystique." Mike Wallace would even use those words in his opening of the *60 Minutes* segment. And Coors knew the dangers of bad press, especially as it related to the union boycott. Now, that training and experience would be put to the ultimate test, an interview for *60 Minutes*, certainly viewed then as the most hostile media environment for business, by the person with the reputation as the toughest interviewer in the business, Mike Wallace. Lisa

Trouble Brewing

and I were asked to come to Golden to join the Coors preparation team.

Golden, Colorado, is a small town snuggled between Denver and the base of the Rocky Mountains. It's one main street is preserved to look much as it did a century ago when the area's chief industry was mining. Today, anyone passing through or around Golden can't miss the chief industry, the huge Coors Brewery. It's surrounded by gently rolling hills, not the snowcapped peaks of the Coors commercials, but they loom to the west, and they feed the cold, clear stream that runs through the brewery and provides the "Rocky Mountain spring water" Coors has made famous. In a virtual war room in the main administration building of the Coors Brewery, Meadows, Richard, Lisa LeMaster and I plotted on flip charts the positives and negatives of the likely *60 Minutes* questions.

From their conversations with the CBS crew and their knowledge of the issues involved in the union's boycott, Richard and Meadows had a good idea of what information was available to *60 Minutes*. Based on our experience in the news business, Lisa and I set out to anticipate what their reactions would be to that information, what approach they would take, what questions Mike Wallace would ask.

We went through the same steps to prepare for *60 Minutes* that we had taken for countless other interviews, perhaps a little more carefully, perhaps with some trepidation, but, if so, it wasn't evident in the war room. Shirley Richard and John Meadows seemed energized. Lisa LeMaster was her usual calm, confident self, moving us step by step through the preparation process. I found it exhilarating. We knew our techniques

3

Chapter One

for preparing for an interview worked, even in the most hostile of circumstances. They had never failed us in dozens of interviews of oil executives during the "energy crisis," of political candidates, of business executives facing what they perceived to be media crises. The only difference was the name and reputation of the program and the interviewer: *60 Minutes* and Mike Wallace, the best, and to most business people, the most fearsome, in their business. We welcomed the opportunity like a young gunfighter in the old West might welcome the opportunity to face off against the gunman with the biggest reputation, and probably with the same dangerous naivete.

We're never so naive, though, as to plunge in without asking why. Why are we doing this? What do we, in this case, Coors, want to accomplish? We don't think it's possible to make a good story out of a bad one—a plane crash, an oil spill. The question we ask is, can we make it better? If *60 Minutes* is going to do a story on the union boycott of Coors, knowing all the bad things the union will say, knowing the tough questions that will be provoked, is there anything positive we can hope to accomplish? Coors had already answered that question from a most practical standpoint. As Joe and Bill Coors would say on the program that finally aired, the boycott was hurting Coors badly, and, from Coors' viewpoint, unfairly. Being able to answer the union allegations on one of the country's highest rated programs was a chance for survival. None of the Coors executives doubted the rightness of their position. All those of us toiling in the war room had to do was make sure they were able to tell their story in the face of Mike Wallace's toughest questions, and tell it in such a way that the *60 Minutes* editors would use it in the final edited program,

Trouble Brewing

knowing that the union's worst charges would certainly be aired as well.

We all knew what the union would say. The AFL-CIO had kept a full-time employee busy making speeches condemning Coors for alleged discrimination against practically everyone in the world. The boycott had been especially effective among college students and gay organizations and was making inroads among African-Americans and Hispanics. The union painted a picture of Coors as a fascist state, where employees surrendered all rights. Our message was simple: "Those charges are not true. Only the union is saying those things, and that is because Coors employees voted out the AFL-CIO in a decertification election."

To get the opportunity to deliver that message on TV, and especially to prove the first point, that the allegations were not true, we first had to be able to answer all the tough questions Mike Wallace would ask. Much of our time in the war room was spent making sure we had the answers. It wasn't difficult to anticipate the questions. From many years on the other side of the microphone, Lisa and I had no difficulty thinking like a news producer or an interviewer, even Mike Wallace. John Meadows and Shirley Richard knew what the union would say, and they had answered most of the allegations many times in public forums.

The union would charge that Coors hiring and employment practices discriminated against women and minorities. They would allege that a pre-employment polygraph test required by Coors asked questions about sexual preferences, setting up possible discrimination against homosexuals. They would paint the picture of a fascist company, routinely searching employees' belongings, firing anyone whose locker, or even car,

Chapter One

might contain evidence of drug use. And, of course, they would charge that Coors was anti-union, keeping an unhappy work force at bay because there was no union to defend those employees' rights. That last was the battle we wanted to fight, but to get there, we had to wade through the a minefield of all the other points.

John and Shirley answered each question firmly and directly. The brewery would be opened to *60 Minutes* to see for themselves the women, Hispanics and African-Americans among the work force.

"We have to be sure they see the fitness center," Shirley said.

John produced an article praising Coors, written recently by a gay journalist, and an award from LULAC, the League of United Latin American Citizens. Both would play a part in the final, televised drama, especially the LULAC award. We would suggest they talk to the person who had been responsible for administering lie detector tests. We would make available a distributor from the Bay Area of California to talk about the effects of the boycott by students and gays organizations.

Selection of an on-camera spokesperson or spokespersons can make or break a media effort. In this case, we all knew who our chief spokespersons would be; not anyone with PR or communications in their title, but Joe and Bill Coors themselves. They were personally the target of the union's attacks. They would be our defenders. We would prepare the sons, Pete and Jeff, as well, the next generation of Coors leadership, but we knew who Mike Wallace would want to talk to.

Where should that interview take place? Should the brothers be interviewed together or separately? What should they wear? Each of those questions was not just

Trouble Brewing

logistical, but tactical. Lisa chose a spot in the library of the old Coors homeplace that still stands on the brewery grounds, a perfect combination of the business and the personal image we hoped would come though. When it was suggested to the *60 Minutes* crew, they loved it. The interview took place in the exact spot Lisa picked, from the angle she suggested, bookcase in the background. Joe and Bill sat comfortably (but not so comfortably as to appear unconcerned) in the chairs Lisa picked for them. Only one thing was changed. She had picked a lower chair for Mike Wallace so he would have to look up slightly, rather than glaring down at his targets. Mike exchanged that chair for another on a level with the brothers.

Joe and Bill asked whether they should wear suits and ties for the interview.

"What do you ordinarily wear to work?" Lisa asked.

"Never coats and ties," Joe said. "This is a brewery, not a bank."

"Then you should do the interview in shirt sleeves," Lisa decided. "We want you to feel natural and comfortable and to look natural and comfortable."

At one point in the program as it aired, Mike Wallace is walking with the two brothers on the brewery grounds. They're wearing light, windbreaker type jackets. People who saw the program, and knew of our involvement, often mentioned that scene and asked me if that was a setup on our part, designed to make the Coors brothers look real and folksy. The answer is unequivocally no. Had they ordinarily worn suits to work, that's what they would have been wearing. Any attempt to concoct an artificial image, in our opinion and experience, only makes the spokesperson uncomfortable and usually appears as artificial as it is.

Chapter One

Our goal is the opposite: to make the real person come through even in the face of hostile questioning.

On our flip chart in the war room, every question had been checked off, each answered to the best of our ability, each matched to a positive response relating to our overall message. We had specific answers to each union charge, including that Coors was anti-union. There was, in fact, another union, although a small one, still representing Coors employees, and it was the employees themselves who had voted out the AFL-CIO. We were secure in our defense, but that wasn't enough. We wanted to make sure that viewers got the whole, true picture of what Coors was all about, and that meant more than just what the Coors brothers would say in their interview.

"We've invited Mike Wallace to attend one of our brown bag lunches," Shirley Richard said.

Each week, Joe or Bill or both would meet with an auditorium full of employees. As informally as the numbers allowed, over brown bag lunches, they listened to whatever gripes the employees might have, and answered any and all questions, no holds barred. They would turn one of these gatherings completely over to Wallace. It would be an unprecedented opportunity for *60 Minutes* to interview all the Coors employees at once, or any individuals they might choose. It could prove everything we wanted to prove about the Coors work force and relationships with management, or it could be a total disaster. Ultimately, the *60 Minutes* editors would decide what to use or not to use from that forum. They would hear what our employees had to say on every touchy issue. Then, CBS would decide what it all meant and which few comments best illustrated those points.

"You seem pretty confident what your employees will

tell Mike," I said.

John Meadows leaned back in his chair and smiled a faint smile.

"We're confident."

All the members of the Coors family who might be interviewed had been through media training in the past few years, but we put them through a refresher, dealing with the anticipated *60 Minutes* questions and getting them to focus on our positive messages. They were all proficient at giving short, honest answers to interviewers' questions and then making their own applicable points. Basically, that's our technique, whether dealing with *60 Minutes* or a local news interview. Unlike most people in our profession, media consultants, crisis consultants, spin doctors, whatever name is applied, we insist that our clients answer questions directly and honestly. Every question, in plain, direct English. Anyone who thinks they can get into some glib word game with Mike Wallace or Sam Donaldson or Barbara Walters and come out ahead is in for a rude awakening. Besides, the public isn't stupid. The audience knows when someone is avoiding questions and all credibility is lost. The Coors brothers' open and honest answers, some surprisingly candid, would prove to be a major positive in the final program.

Shirley Richard, Lisa LeMaster and I went over our check list to confirm we had done everything we could think of to prepare—messages, answers to every anticipated question, spokespersons selected and prepared, interview location chosen, other supporting interview possibilities suggested to *60 Minutes*, written backup material prepared and, in most cases already in the hands of the producer. Now it was time to open the

Chapter One

gates to Mike Wallace.

Wallace did at least four hours of interviews at the brewery. We have that much on video tape in our office, tape made by the camera crew Coors provided at our suggestion to duplicate *60 Minutes'* footage. We routinely suggest that a separate tape be made of any interview, so we have a complete, unedited version. In some cases they have proved useful in distributing information after the fact to other media. We recognize that their main purpose is to serve as a security blanket for executives who fear being taken out of context in the final edit.

That four hours doesn't count footage of Wallace strolling the grounds with Joe and Bill, of the wellness center, of various photogenic assembly lines of bottles being filled with foamy, golden liquid, or of plant security guards, all of which ended up on the finished program. Nor does it include interviews Wallace conducted at other locations such as union headquarters, a San Francisco gay bar, the home of a fired Coors employee. It does include an hour with Joe and Bill, two hours at the brown bag luncheon with employees, and an hour of Coors employees in other settings. From all that, the finished segment on CBS ran a total of 16 minutes. From their hour interview, Joe and Bill Coors were on the air for 2 minutes and 18 seconds in seven segments that ranged in length from 10 seconds to 32 seconds.

The scariest days are those spent waiting for the program to be edited and aired. Shirley Richard had reported to us each step of the way, what *60 Minutes* had decided to tape ("People working out at the wellness center! Yesss!"), and how the actual interviews had

Trouble Brewing

appeared to go (Brown bag dinner, scary, long, content seemed good; Coors interview, great, right on target). Even without knowing what the other side had said or shown to Wallace, we didn't see how the piece could come out less than a draw, but we weren't in it to break even. The biggest concern Lisa and I had, the biggest we usually have, was whether we had managed to make our side of the story exciting enough. "Boycott." "Discrimination." "Fascists." Those are exciting words, news words. Could we match them? The game now narrowed, as it always does when dealing with media, to one of choices. Had we offered what Mike Wallace and producer Alan Maraynes would be looking for when they edited the segment?

Lisa and I were watching in Dallas when the familiar *60 Minutes* stopwatch logo ticked into a picture of Mike Wallace in front of the segment title, "Trouble Brewing." His opening words laid out the story's devastating premise: "...stories that the Coors company is anti-black, anti-woman, anti-homosexual...and that's just for starters. There are also stories that Coors treats its employees shabbily, inhumanely..."

Examination of these charges went on for 2 minutes and 40 seconds before there was any Coors response. Bill Coors branded the charges an "unprincipled attack" by the union.

"They're out to destroy us."

Touchdown for our side!

Our team had scored the first time it touched the ball. In a twenty second statement, Bill Coors had defined the battle in our terms.

But the ball went back to the other side. Wallace ran down a list of all the charges again, reading from a union boycott flier. The segment was six minutes old

Chapter One

before the "bad news" ended. Then it was back to the Coors brothers and Bill Coors telling Wallace, "Our books are open to anybody, Mike...I know of no company other than ours that has completely open books to anybody."

"Coors opened its books to us...," responded Wallace, flipping the pages of a loose leaf binder covered in red. He began to go down the list of charges one more time, but this time giving the Coors response. The book Mike had "opened" was a PR manual, prepared by Coors' corporate communications department to address the boycott issues. The next ten minutes saw an avalanche bury the union's arguments.

The issue of treating employees badly was addressed by showing pictures of the wellness center, with employees, including women and African-Americans, running on a track and otherwise working out. Bill Coors was asked whether questions about sexual preference had been asked on pre-employment polygraph tests. He answered truthfully.

"I don't know, Mike. There was a period when we didn't know what questions were asked."

Cut to an interview with the man whose firm had done the testing for Coors, who said flatly, "Those questions were not asked."

In response to charges of discrimination against minorities, Wallace mentioned that LULAC, the League of Latin American Citizens, was giving an award to Coors. It produced the beginning of an on-camera deterioration of David Sickler, the former Coors employee now paid by the AFL-CIO to run the boycott, that was worthy of Captain Queeg in *The Caine Mutiny*.

"We think that's a damned shame."

"Why are they getting all these awards, then?"

Trouble Brewing

"Money, Mike...they contribute lots and lots of money."

Then, the brown bag lunch, Mike Wallace sitting alone on the front edge of a stage, in an auditorium filled with hundreds of Coors employees. Wallace selected employees at random to respond to the various union charges of discrimination and ill-treatment.

An Hispanic employee identified as a supervisor says he has been with Coors for 18 years.

"Coors was hiring Hispanics before it was fashionable."

A woman says she has been with Coors 23 years. The camera moves to a closeup of a petite woman next to her who wants to respond to allegations that Coors is "anti-people".

"Coors is pro-people, 100 per cent."

The camera, still in closeup, pans down to the woman's side where she is holding a hard hat.

"What kind of hard-hat job do you have?" Wallace asks.

"Construction supervisor."

Watching this on a Sunday evening at home in Dallas, I found myself exhaling a long breath and leaning back in my chair. I hadn't realized that I was leaning forward intently, virtually holding my breath up to then. But now I knew it was all over, no matter what happened in the last couple of minutes.

We hadn't just dodged the *60 Minutes* bullets. We had won.

Wallace asked the assembled employees how many had taken pre-employment polygraph tests. A wide shot of the audience showed every hand go up. Wallace asked how many had been asked questions about their

Chapter One

sexual preferences. Dramatically, every hand went down.

There was one major question that had still not been addressed, the allegation that Coors routinely launched searches of employees belongings, looking for drugs, which were absolutely prohibited on company property. This one was beyond our control. John Meadows and Shirley Richard knew that *60 Minutes* was going to interview an employee, one Jerry Burella, who had been fired when security guards found the stub of what appeared to be a marijuana cigarette in the ashtray of his pickup truck. They knew, because the producer told them. We didn't know what Burella might say. He described the search and launched into a defense of Coors' right to make the rules as long as they write the checks.

"Coors is known to be one of the best places to work in Denver."

All that remained was for Mike Wallace to drive the last nail into the coffin and tie it with a black ribbon. He had done it with flair for a dozen years, and would for at least that many more.

Across the desk from Sickler, Wallace asked if he could name an incident in the last five years in which abusive questions had been asked on a polygraph exam. Sickler said he could not.

"But as long as they administer those tests, the potential for abuse is there."

Wallace noted that "a whole lot" of other companies required polygraph tests, "and you're not boycotting them."

"That's right Mike," Sickler said, "and most of those companies have union contracts."

Watching at home, I know my mouth fell open and I

was back on the edge of my seat. I couldn't believe what I had heard. Wallace raised an index finger that reminded me of Charlton Heston as Moses raising the staff of God.

"That really is the nub of the issue. They got rid of the union."

"That's right."

Now back to the Coors brothers for the epitaph. Wallace suggests that the boycott is hurting Coors, or the brothers wouldn't have agreed to face his questioning. Bill Coors agrees. The final word is left to Joe Coors.

"We want the truth of the Coors story known to the American public."

Coors was so pleased with the outcome that they ran newspaper ads quoting *60 Minutes* on Coors. Finally, they bought the rights to reproduce the segment and distributed several hundred copies themselves.

In a book called *Talking Back to the Media*, published in 1986, author Peter Hannaford said "The *60 Minutes* segment that aired turned out to be a major public relations plus for the Adolph Coors Company."

Roger Ailes, media consultant to George Bush and Dan Quayle in their successful campaign, in his 1988 book, *You Are the Message*, said, "The *60 Minutes* segment ...turned out to be a major public relations boost for Coors."

Ailes makes it clear, though, that he thinks the Coors story is an anomaly. He flatly says he would be very reluctant to suggest that one of his clients go on *60 Minutes*. That's unfortunate. The lesson of Coors is that someone with a true story to tell, properly prepared to

Chapter One

tell it, can do just that in any media interview, including *60 Minutes*. Of course we didn't know in 1982 that we would have so many opportunities to prove that. We thought our experience with Coors and *60 Minutes* was probably the high point of our careers as media consultants.

It was only the beginning.

Lessons learned from Coors

There is no substitute for preparation. All the glibness or clever messages in the world would not have been as helpful as the information gathered by John Meadows and Shirley Richard. All the planning that goes into a political campaign went into preparing for *60 Minutes*.

Expect the toughest questions. It does no good to hope something won't be asked. It probably will.

Think of more than just the interview. Because the Coors brothers were well prepared to handle the Mike Wallace interview, we were able to deal with other aspects of the program, suggesting other angles to be followed, other people to be interviewed, supplying written information and background material.

Even the president of the company can say "I don't know." Bill Coors proved it when asked about questions included in polygraph tests. First, it was true, he hadn't known the specific questions. Second, we sure didn't want him fighting that battle. Because he said "I don't know," we were able to get the question directed to the proper person to answer it, the head of the firm that administered the tests.

Chapter One

Don't try to fake it. It's tough enough to get the opportunity for a real person to tell a true story. To try to create a false image or to make a phony story credible imposes obstacles that are insurmountable. We have been asked, often in awed tones, how we got *60 Minutes* to show all those pictures of African-Americans and women, to interview the woman in the hard hat and the Hispanic veteran of 18 years with the company. The answer is, we didn't. We couldn't have. They had to be there and they had to be real, but given that, we could be pretty sure CBS would use them. The union made sure of that by insisting there were no women, African-Americans or Hispanics at Coors. That insured that *60 Minutes* would find them if they were there. Then the *60 Minutes* editors simply picked out the best and most quotable.

Chapter Two

Soul Searching and Ambush Journalism

The Coors segment on *60 Minutes* drew a good deal of attention from business *and* the media. It was generally viewed as a victory for the business "target", and that was something that just didn't happen. Coors talked publicly about the program, even buying newspaper ads with the headline "The four most dreaded words in the English language: 'Mike Wallace is here.'" We still have one of those framed, hanging in our office. Our kind of media consulting had been around for ten years, since the Arab oil embargo forced oil companies to change their attitudes about dealing with the media, particularly television. I had been involved from the beginning. Somehow, though, when the media finally became aware that this was going on— this strange concept of business executives who were going to be interviewed actually preparing for it, actually

Chapter Two

having something to say and being able to say it— the media found the thought totally alien. The idea caused no little soul searching on the media's part.

I know of no industry that likes to soul search more than media. They're in the business, after all, of looking into people's souls, letting us know daily who are the bad guys and good guys in our towns, our country and our world; and they don't hesitate to do it to themselves. Over many years as a radio and television news director, I attended countless seminars of the Radio/Television News Directors Association, Associated Press or United Press International Broadcasters Association, and various state associations, at which the prime topics were our own shortcomings. These discussions often involved questions about media coverage of business. In the '70s and into the '80s there was a trend toward hiring "business news editors" at the networks and some individual radio and TV stations. This was in direct response to growing criticism, some prompted by concerns about *60 Minutes*, that the media were inherently anti-business. Most of those "business editors" did little more than read daily stock market results, and the practice has all but gone away, but it illustrates media sensitivity to criticism.

Whether involving business coverage or coverage of the President of the United States, most of the complaints against the media boiled down to their negativism. "You're always out after the negative." "You're only looking for the sensational." "It's only news if its bad news." The average reader or viewer, thinking the media see themselves as above criticism, would be amazed to know how much concern those charges have provoked within the media. I, with several other news directors, spent some pleasant hours over drinks in a

Soul Searching and Ambush Journalism

Miami hotel following one news directors' convention, discussing those issues with Sam Donaldson, who was just about to become White House correspondent for ABC. There was very little disagreement, and no proposed solutions, as I recall. The point is that media people hear the criticism and are concerned. Like all of us, they would like to be loved.

The reaction of some media people after the Coors *60 Minutes* segment seemed to suggest that CBS had been flummoxed, had somehow lost its journalistic integrity because its victims had actually *prepared* to be interviewed and *60 Minutes* knew it, or should have. *60 Minutes'* response was to do a program on the subject of the role of media consultants. It was called "Camera Shy," and was hosted by Mike Wallace. Lisa and I were not invited. The panelists were a few media consultants based in New York and Boston, easy for CBS to find, lending credence to another media criticism, that it's hard for them to take seriously anything west of the Hudson. We thought those who were invited, though, did a very good job of representing our relatively young profession.

One of the panelists was my former partner, Jack Hilton. He certainly should have been there. He was the single person most responsible for creating "spokesperson training" at the request of the major oil companies ten years earlier. He hired me to be a part of that first training program while I was host of a news-talk radio program in New York, and later he and I formed the first consulting firm to specialize full-time in media training. Hilton asked Mike Wallace about *his* reaction to any business person who had the courage to go on a program like *60 Minutes*. Wallace replied, "How

21

Chapter Two

can I hate you for coming on television and being honest?"

Perhaps because he had been stung a little by media reaction to Coors' preparation, but more likely simply because it's his style, Wallace took an adversarial position. He suggested several times that the technique of preparation offered a "potential for its being misused." He said the object appeared to be to "put a good face on bad news."

Another panelist was Arnold Zenker, a former CBS news employee who left the media to start a consulting business after achieving one flare of national fame as the newscaster who filled in for Walter Cronkite when Cronkite once stayed off the air during a strike by union newscasters and announcers. Zenker gave an impressive explanation of why his new profession was necessary.

"The truth of the matter is that the public relations vice president isn't likely to say to the chairman of the board, 'You are a bore.' You need a hired gun to do that. You need an outsider...to come in and say, 'You know, that's sort of dull—and dull doesn't work well on television.'"

The program spent a good deal of time on a side issue probably of interest only to the media themselves, the question of whether it was ethical for active news people to help in such training. Edwin Newman, who had occasionally made appearances with Hilton and me to share his expertise with business people, thought it was. He said what he told them was up to him, not anything he had been asked to say. Leslie Stahl, many years away from becoming a *60 Minutes* correspondent herself, said she had helped with some training for "the State Department," and she obviously regretted doing it.

Soul Searching and Ambush Journalism

She felt she had helped train them "to tell less than the whole truth." The program produced no specific consensus, other than that it was bad for anyone to lie, even to the media, but that it was probably all right (Leslie Stahl dissenting) to think before blurting out one's thoughts to a national TV audience. One *60 Minutes* producer appeared on the program, Alan Maraynes, who had produced the Coors segment. That wasn't mentioned. Maraynes asked and answered a question himself.

"Are we simply trying to catch people off guard? No. I think this sort of thing elevates the art form to a certain extent."

Not long after that program, I saw a quote from Mike Wallace in some in-flight magazine that seemed to agree with Maraynes, and which I have chosen to believe reflects Wallace's real opinion. He said, quoting as best I can remember, "If we, the networks, and they, business, and the public, all want the same thing—for American business to tell its story to the public—then we should applaud anything that makes that possible."

Around that same time, *60 Minutes* did another introspective piece called "Looking at *60 Minutes*." It involved a panel of experts, some from media, some from business, discussing several issues with Wallace and with the creator and executive producer of *60 Minutes*, Don Hewitt. Wallace introduced one segment as a discussion of:

"Confrontation journalism, or the so-called ambush interview —though we've done comparatively little of it ourselves on *60 Minutes*."

Wallace described the technique as one in which a reporter "surprises his quarry (interesting choice of

23

Chapter Two

words for an impartial journalist!) on the street or in his office."

This might happen, he explained, because the reporter "has been turned down or has reason to believe he might be turned down" in a request for an interview.

Then came a series of pieces proving that *60 Minutes*, whether or not the most prolific practitioner of the ambush interview, had certainly raised it to an art form. There was Mike himself, trench coat (yes, Holy Cliches, trench coat) flapping in the breeze as he darted across a street in pursuit of his "quarry," who evidently had sold some questionable franchises. Even mild-mannered Harry Reasoner, whose disposition made him as much a candidate for Andy Rooney's job as for Wallace's, was represented, walking into a camera store that had allegedly sold bootleg video tapes to a *60 Minutes* producer. Morley Safer, himself not generally thought of as one of *60 Minutes'* attack dogs, was shown trying to interview a plastic surgeon hurrying along a sidewalk while Safer, in voice over, details his history of malpractice suits.

The panel quickly got to the point, asking Hewitt if it is possible to say "no" to a *60 Minutes* interview.

Hewitt responded that this was "the only way you get to see the man about whom we're doing the story. We don't chase them..."

The panel pointed out that they had just seen at least two instances that looked suspiciously like chases.

"I'm going to surprise you," Hewitt responded. "I agree with you. I think this is probably a technique that has been abused and I have a feeling that we shouldn't be trying to get people to talk to us who obviously don't want to talk. In fact what you're asking a man to do is to testify against himself. You shouldn't do that."

Soul Searching and Ambush Journalism

We have to forgive Don Hewitt if he got carried away and went further than he intended, perhaps speaking in hyperbole because he was in front of those probing *60 Minutes* cameras. It has happened to many. It seemed like the thing to say at the time. But this segment, like all *60 Minutes* segments was taped and edited for broadcast, the choice quotes picked out for air. Unlike most who appear on *60 Minutes*, Hewitt had plenty of time and opportunity to look at it and say, "Wait a minute, I didn't mean that. Don't put that on the air." Thus, we must assume that Hewitt looked at it and said, as Bill Coors had said in response to a Mike Wallace question about his feeling that union's are simply a result of bad management, "That's right, Mike. I said it, and I meant it."

If Hewitt did "have a feeling that we shouldn't be trying to get people to talk to us who obviously don't want to talk..." then he managed to put those feelings behind him. "Confrontation journalism" has remained a mainstay of *60 Minutes* and has been copied by all its clones. On July 2, 1995, in a rerun of a program from 1994, Leslie Stahl appeared to corner U. S. Senator Dennis Diconcini at a public function, then followed him along a sidewalk in a replay of what we had seen described as ambush on the "Looking at *60 Minutes*" program ten years earlier. Diconcini made it clear that he was not interested in talking to Stahl. He told her to get lost. She kept after him, of course.

Perhaps Hewitt's philosophy on testifying against oneself didn't extend to public officials, but there have been consistent examples of the same techniques continuing to be used against ordinary business people as well. The question still arises, then, "Is it possible to

Chapter Two

say 'no' to a *60 Minutes* interview?"

The answer to that question deserves, and will get, a chapter to itself.

Soul Searching and Ambush Journalism

Avoiding the ambush

Don't run. Don't hide; Don't put your hand in front of the camera. Don Hewitt's protestations not withstanding, the ambush interview accomplishes nothing except making the victim look guilty. These knee-jerk responses only help do that. Our advice is, if confronted by any news camera, stay calm. Ask, on camera, "What is this about?" No matter what the response, tell the reporter you don't do interviews on the street (or in the hallway, or at the meeting of the Garden Club).

If there is a legitimate reason for not being interviewed, say so. I'm not the person you need to be talking to. I need more facts before I start responding on camera. Look, I'm really uncomfortable talking to you out here. Let me go change the pants I just wet and I'll consider doing an interview.

If an interview has been declined previously, tell them why. As my secretary told you when you called.... As you know, my attorney is handling all contact with the media. This is not our story. You need to talk to someone else.

Stick with it. The reporter may never be satisfied with your response, but don't panic. *Assume you will be on the air* and think how your response will look to the *real audience*.

27

Chapter Two

> **And the best way to avoid an ambush, be available (but be prepared).** Remember Mike Wallace's rationale for the ambush. The target is someone who has turned down an interview or that the reporter thinks *might* turn one down.

Chapter Three

A Time Bomb on Every Corner

We received a call one Tuesday in December 1983, from Les Rogers, head of media relations for Exxon, U. S. A., based in Houston.

"Can you and Lisa be here tomorrow? Harry Reasoner is going to be here Friday."

We usually have more notice than that when *60 Minutes* is involved. We've never had less. They generally work several weeks, even months, ahead, except when a breaking news story is involved. That wasn't the case here, but, for whatever reason, we were on a very short fuse.

"Reasoner is going to interview our vice president responsible for lust," we were told when we arrived at the company's building in downtown Houston.

"I beg your pardon," I said. "You have a vice president for lust?"

Chapter Three

"LUST. All capitals. Leaking underground storage tanks."

That's the first I had heard about a problem that would get much more publicity in the next few years. In most cities in America, there were service stations on virtually every major corner, in some cases on all four corners of the same intersection. Now we were learning that the huge underground tanks that held the gasoline until it was pumped into your car's gas tank were getting old and rusty. In some cases they were beginning to leak. LUST. At best the problem threatened pollution of water supplies. At worst, the leaks could be a fire hazard with the possibility of explosion.

While our client had to assume that *60 Minutes* might go into the apocalyptic implications of a time bomb on every corner of America's cities, the specific story they were ostensibly covering was simpler. It involved a small community in Rhode Island, where gasoline had seeped into the public water supply. Officials assumed it had come from a leaking tank belonging to one of two competing service stations located on corners diagonally across from each other. The problem had gotten so bad that the public water supply was unusable. While trying to find the source of the leak, the two oil companies that owned the stations were providing bottled water to affected residents.

"I can imagine the pictures," Lisa said. "Mothers bathing their babies in tubs of bottled water heated on the kitchen stove."

"Where will you be doing the interview?" she asked.

The answer was that it would take place in the basement of the Exxon building, where the company had a complete, state-of-the-art TV studio, probably better equipped than any real TV station in town.

A Time Bomb on Every Corner

"Why would you do that?" Lisa asked. "In the first place, why would *60 Minutes* want to send Harry Reasoner to Houston to do an interview in a TV studio that looks just like any in New York? More importantly, who's going to appear in control? Your vice president, or Harry Reasoner, who spends his life in a TV studio? Who's going to *be* in control?"

Les Rogers was smart and experienced. A former United Press International reporter, he had been at Exxon a long time and would retire there. He was among the handful of oil company PR people who, in the early '70s, had recognized the need for some kind of program to train executives to deal with the media and had helped J. Walter Thompson create one. Everyone in the "spokesperson training" business literally owed their careers to him. He had a reason for wanting to tape this interview in the basement studio. This was at the time when the TV show "Dallas" was at the height of its popularity. Les had visions of the *60 Minutes* cameras panning the Houston skyline from the plush office of an oil company vice president.

"Let's go look at his office," Lisa said.

High up in the building, with what was indeed a panoramic view of the Houston skyline, Lisa looked around a fairly large, but otherwise unnotable, office.

"My guess is," she said, "that Harry Reasoner's office is at least as plush as this, but if you're nervous, let's see about a conference room or something of the sort on this floor. I just think the last thing you want is to do it in the TV studio."

She explained that it was not just for looks.

"The key is for him (the vice president) to *be* comfortable. Then he'll look comfortable and that has a lot to do with credibility. You don't want him thinking

Chapter Three

about the physical setup, only what he wants to say."

We agreed that they would suggest using a conference room adjacent to the office of the chosen spokesperson, Senior Vice President Ed Hess. Since Hess had already been through media training, and because of the time limitations, we spent just a short while with him, going over objectives and questions that would probably be asked.

Again, we have the backup tape the client made of the entire interview, not just what was aired. Ed Hess and Harry Reasoner are seated facing each other toe to toe, on the same side of the conference table, between the table and a credenza. *60 Minutes* has two cameras, each positioned to shoot one of the participants head on. In the finished product, oilman and Reasoner would never appear together, each shown from the front, individually.

The first five minutes of the interview were devoted to the overall question of LUST and how bad the potential problem might be. Hess said Exxon had 26,000 underground gasoline tanks in 7,000 locations around the country. He talked about the company's extensive program to upgrade the tanks, cited a huge amount of money being spent on the program and said he expected 100% of the tanks to be replaced by 1986.

Then Reasoner turned specifically to questions about the apparent leak that had contaminated drinking water in Rhode Island. Hess expressed concern about the problem and factually answered the questions. Ten minutes into the interview, someone on the *60 Minutes* crew interrupted, asking for a pause to reload video tape. That will happen in every *60 Minutes* interview. I have seen the "reloading" break come at thirty minutes into an interview that was scheduled for an hour, and

A Time Bomb on Every Corner

an hour into an interview that was going two hours. I have no doubt that there really is a need for changing tapes and that the difference in time may be attributed to different lengths of tape being used, but I caution that these breaks are also used for quick conferences between talent (the interviewer) and producer concerning weak spots that should be probed further. It should be viewed as an opportunity for interviewees to review their positions, too, not with an eye toward expanding objectives, but toward making sure they stay on track after the break.

In this case, after the tape change, Reasoner went back over some of the same ground and asked for a little bit of speculation on blame which was not forthcoming. Then, after three and a half minutes, Reasoner himself asked for another break. After a brief conference, he came back with what he defined as "technical questions" about the company's procedures for repairing or replacing leaking tanks. At one point, Ed Hess reached across the table to pick up a large manual of procedures to illustrate his answers. That would not have been possible had the interview taken place in the TV studio. The third part of the interview lasted one minute, 41 seconds. Total time of the interview, just over 15 minutes, compared with four hours of Mike Wallace at Coors. It would be enough. Our part of the actual program would be one minute and seven seconds.

It was titled "Check the Water." It began with Reasoner describing the problem of leaking tanks as what the Environmental Protection Agency said could be "the major pollution problem of the 80s." We all used to know our neighborhood service station owner, Reasoner

Chapter Three

said, and used to ask him about any problems with our cars. "You probably didn't ask him," he said, "if he had buried a time bomb in your neighborhood."

The focus quickly turned to the small community in Rhode Island, where, Reasoner said, the problem had existed for 14 years! It had begun with one family reporting that its tap water had started to taste like gasoline. Finally, an entire subdivision of 15 families had similar complaints. There were Reasoner interviews with residents, the local fire chief, and a former president of the town council trying to explain why the problem hadn't been solved in 14 years. The only answer the former town official gave was that he had been told it wouldn't do any good to sue a big oil company.

The only oil company mentioned so far was *not* our client, but the company that owned the other service station, diagonally across the street. Now that company's executive vice president got his first chance to respond.

"We have had no history of a leak at that station...The hydrocarbon that is in the water aquifer...I don't think is (our) hydrocarbon."

Then came more residents, one talking about being "shuttled from agency to agency..." a mother of three daughters who "can't take a shower after basketball. They have to take a sponge bath."

About six minutes into what would be a thirteen-and-a-half minute piece, we had seen a perfect example of why business people sometimes *don't* win on *60 Minutes*. The issue was highly emotional, and especially so on television. Lisa's worst fears of how it would be portrayed had already been realized, a time bomb on every corner, children bathing in bottled water. But the

34

A Time Bomb on Every Corner

worst damage, in my opinion, came from the juxtaposition of all that with a business spokesperson denying the existence of the problem and denying it in jargon that conveyed a lack of feeling or understanding. The mothers, the fire chief, a lawyer who had filed a $100 million lawsuit, didn't talk about hydrocarbons in the aquifer. They talked about drinking water that smelled like gasoline, of showers that couldn't be taken, and sponge baths that had to be. Their emotion couldn't be answered by anything anyone might say about hydrocarbons and aquifers.

This is not meant to say the other company's spokesperson didn't do a good job, from their point of view. He was stating their case strongly and in terms that obviously were quotable enough to make the *60 Minutes* cut. But someone had apparently chosen to fight what we considered the wrong battle, denying the problem, and they had chosen to do it in words guaranteed not to be believed by anyone outside their industry. I'm sure he thought he was being responsive, and perhaps he *was* being responsive to Reasoner's questions, but he did not appear to be responsive to the residents' problem. The result was what people describe when they ask why any business person would go on *60 Minutes*. The "other side" was portrayed as victims, the business representative as unfeeling, uncaring and totally defensive.

They're right. That's exactly what happened. But *60 Minutes* didn't do it. It was totally the company's fault. In fact, it was the company's *choice*. They must have chosen to say the problem didn't exist, and if it did exist it wasn't their fault. They chose to talk about hydrocarbons and aquifers instead of gasoline in the drinking water. We could rarely find an example like

35

Chapter Three

this, where we can compare the comments of two different company vice presidents from the same industry taking such different approaches to the same questions.

Six minutes into the program, Reasoner went back to the bigger picture. "Is this an isolated case?" he asked an "expert." The expert claimed that 75,000 tanks may be leaking right now.

Back to the same executive vice president again denying the problem, only even more strongly.

"Except for human error, we don't have *any* leaks in our tanks!"

The first comment from our spokesperson, Hess, came eight minutes into the program when Reasoner finally pointed out that there were two service stations involved, both trying to find the leak.

"We don't believe our station is responsible for the gasoline components in the underground water."

After comments from an elderly woman who couldn't lift the bottles, and a mother worried about whether the water might have caused a birth defect in her child, another woman showed what she has to go through to heat water simply to wash her face.

Ten minutes and forty-eight seconds into the program, Harry Reasoner said, "Although (the first oil company) thinks this is an isolated case, Exxon is less sure."

"Harry, we're very concerned about the problem..." and Ed Hess talked about $100 million already spent on solving the problem of leaking tanks and said 100% of Exxon's tanks will be replaced by 1986.

The final word from the other company spokesperson was strong and positive as well, talking about fiber glass

A Time Bomb on Every Corner

tanks his company had used to replace old ones, but the ending to the program could only be viewed in light of his earlier comments.

"While we were reporting this program," Reasoner said, "(that company) discovered and reported a leak..."

The final pictures were of a backhoe digging up their service station and an official saying the station had been ordered closed.

I didn't watch the program when it aired on CBS, only a videotape later. As usual, we were on to other crises. WE knew that our man had done well and that it was unlikely there could be any bad results, no matter how he was edited. Not until much later did I realize that the job he did in the interview, and the results on the air for Exxon, were every bit as good as the Coors results. In a little over 15 minutes of interview he had hit all his objectives and had not been drawn into other areas. In the thirteen-and-one-half minutes of the actual program, three segments were used, 10, 25 and 32 seconds long, a total of one minute and seven seconds. Every one of them spoke to the company's concern for the residents and efforts to solve the problem, including expenditures of $100 million dollars.

You can't do better than that.

Why, then, isn't that program written up in text books as the same kind of triumph Coors was? I guess it's because there were two oil companies involved, not just one, so it was not a clear cut victory for business. But judged by the success of handling the interview and getting exactly the right comments chosen by the editors, it was a total success.

Chapter Three

Lessons learned from LUST

Acknowledge the problem. Denial never helps. This doesn't mean taking ownership of the problem or accepting blame (usually the fear of the corporate attorney), but recognizing the problem from the other point of view, in this case, that of the residents.

Express concern. They're opposed to gasoline in their water and not being able to shower. Do we have to be in favor of those things? Absolutely not. We don't have to let ourselves be put in the role of bad guy.

Pick your battle. Our fight was not with the residents, trying to prove them wrong. Our battle was against LUST and *with* the residents to get the problem solved.

Chapter Four

Saying No

Many of those who have writen about *60 Minutes* have cited the Coors program as unique, a rare or *only* time that business has come out ahead. That's definitely not the case. Most companies and individuals we've worked with have come out better than fifty-fifty, and several have scored big, like Coors. Nor do I mean to claim that this is true only of those we work with. A smaller percentage of *60 Minutes* programs are hatchet jobs than most might believe. But not all our exposures to *60 Minutes* have followed this scenario: accept the invitation to appear; prepare diligently; do a brilliant job and then sit back and watch another triumph on Sunday evening. In some cases we have suggested that clients decline the honor of a *60 Minutes* interview. In still others, the interview ended up on the cutting room floor because CBS decided there was no story there. To

Chapter Four

some businesses, that's the best victory of all.

Is it possible to say "no" to *60 Minutes*, to decline an "invitation" to be interviewed without being depicted on the program as a criminal pleading the fifth amendment? The answer is yes, if....

The McDonald's Corporation has asked us several times to help them decide how to respond to a request for an interview by *60 Minutes*, and in several cases that response has been "no, thanks." The first thing we want to know is who contacted them and what they were told about the subject of the program. That first contact has usually been from a producer, in the early stages of putting a segment together. We learned early in our exposure to *60 Minutes* that the producer is key. In later years, we developed an extensive file on the producers, indicating the kind of programs they specialized in, propensity for what we call "dirty tricks," and the correspondent with whom they usually worked. From that information, we can deduce almost everything we need to know about the style of the segment and the interview. Will it be hostile or friendly? Fairly balanced or one-sided?

The first time McDonald's asked, though, we hadn't accumulated that information. We had to rely on contacts from our former media days to check out the producer. From sources at CBS in New York, we were able to learn the title and subject of her most recent effort, and that she had formerly worked in Washington. From friends in Washington media, we gained some information about the producer and her personal style. Then we talked to a media relations person at a company that had been involved in that recent program. Our message to McDonald's was that our checking

Saying No

indicated that this producer's work was professional, generally fair, and relatively non-confrontational.

McDonald's decided to cooperate with *60 Minutes*, supplying a good deal of information, but ended up not being interviewed. While the story involved the "fast food" industry, it only peripherally involved McDonald's. There were better sources for the information CBS needed on camera, and McDonald's helped them find those sources. We learned from that experience that one way to say no to *60 Minutes* was to prove that "it's not our story." That was the answer to several later inquiries to McDonald's. Because the hamburger giant is typical (arch-typical, one might say) of so many facets of American life, they are constantly being asked to comment on things that have nothing to do with hamburgers: nutritional issues, of course, but also chlorofluorocarbons and the ozone layer (because of styrofoam cups), depletion of Brazilian rain forests (because of a rumor that McDonald's was using exotic wood in its restaurants and another that involved South American beef), clubbing baby seals (a vague connection with an Arctic fish supplier), the minimum wage, effects of working on high school students' grades, and so on.

It became a fairly standard answer to *60 Minutes* and other media. "That's just not a McDonald's story." But that answer alone would not always be sufficient. It was followed, whenever possible, by, "but let us help you find someone who can talk about..." nutrition, the ozone layer, or the minimum wage. The result, to the media's satisfaction, was usually a better, more pertinent interview. Of course it didn't hurt our cause that we were able to recommend the experts.

One message here is, if you're going to say "no" to *60*

Chapter Four

Minutes, or any other media interviews, you'd better explain why, and the reason has to be better than "We don't want to," or "We're afraid you won't treat us right." Responses like this say to the media, "We're afraid of what you might ask us." That, in turn, translates into "We're afraid of what you might find out." That says guilty, and so may the result on television. In a segment on the effect of power lines on cattle, Ed Bradley said an electric company spokesperson "declined our request for an interview. A company spokesperson said an on-camera interview 'would make our officials uncomfortable.'" You can imagine that Bradley's tone of voice when he said that was not especially sympathetic.

Usually, though, there is no explanation of why, when the *60 Minutes* correspondent, sometimes standing outside the company's building or an executive's office with nameplate on the door, delivers the one line condemnation.

"No one on the other side would talk to us," says Leslie Stahl, referring to the tobacco lobby.

"Neither Wasserman nor MCA board members would talk with us on camera," says Bradley, after clearly implying collusion with the Mafia.

And Steve Kroft, in a segment called "Bug Man," about using beneficial insects to replace insecticides, left no doubt who the bad guys were when he said the Food and Drug Administration would not comment. "We've been waiting for months for them to return our phone calls."

That certain implication of guilt is one reason we urge companies strongly to consider telling their story on camera, if they truly have a story. In one case we worked with a defense contractor, one of our oldest and most valued clients, that was contacted by *60 Minutes*

Saying No

about a segment concerning one of their subcontractors. The sub, a maker of transducers used in a missile built by our client, had been found guilty a considerable time before of falsifying test information. The guilty officials of the subcontracting company were in prison. It was old news. The only new aspect of the story was that a committee of the U. S. Congress chaired by Michigan Congressman John Dingell, had taken a look at the situation and Dingell's staff had evidently fed the story to *60 Minutes*. This would not be the only time we were called upon to help on a *60 Minutes* story that originated in Congressman Dingell's office.

This was 1989. By then we had compiled a pretty good dossier on producers, but the man in charge of this story was new at CBS. He had recently come over from ABC and *20/20* where, we were told, he specialized in Defense Department stories. Sources in Washington media and at the Department of Defense called him "tough."

We felt fairly secure in our client's position. The company's own testing had, in fact, uncovered the problem and led to conviction of those responsible. We were the victims of whatever fraud took place. No parts had ever failed. But there was the possibility that some untested parts had gotten into finished missiles; not faulty, necessarily, but untested. There was the chance, however remote, that one of those untested parts might fail in battle. That made it a story.

The producer assured the defense contractor's media relations contact that our part of the story was small, that our company was viewed as a victim, but insisted that an interview with one of our executives and access to pictures and information at the missile plant were

Chapter Four

indispensable to his story. Fairchild/LeMaster urged cooperation, including doing an interview. The president of the company, with whom we had worked for several years, agreed.

"If someone is going to tell our story on *60 Minutes*," he said, "it should to be us."

The media relations person agreed only in part. He saw the need to cooperate by providing CBS with answers to specific questions and information about the missile in question, but balked at the idea of an on-camera spokesperson. He was a former Marine Corps public information officer. One of our own associates is a former military PIO, and I respect the job they do under sometimes adverse circumstances. But the military environment offers far greater opportunity to say "no comment," than does the private sector. It provides opportunity to establish and enforce rules for media coverage that don't exist in the outside world where the media make their own rules.

Even within their controlled environment, the military are often shocked at their inability to make the media play by their rules. Our associate, retired army captain Doug Frey, was public information officer at the time of the Reagan-era invasion of the Caribbean island of Grenada. He got the assignment, he says, when the general in charge of the invasion, having landed on the island, contacted Washington.

"I can handle the Cubans here," he said. "I can handle the Russians. But send me someone to handle the (censored) media!"

It was easy to establish the ground rules for CBS cameras taping at the missile plant. They recognized and respected the need for secrecy in that situation. A few days before the CBS crew was scheduled to arrive, I

Saying No

went to the plant and met with all the managers who were going to be made available to answer questions off camera. We planned exactly how to explain to *60 Minutes* what could and could not be videotaped, what questions could and could not be answered. That part went smoothly.

I was still arguing that we should do an on-camera interview. If the producer was telling the truth when he said we were not a target in this story, all we had to do was support that position and not say anything stupid that would make us a target. I knew the company and its spokespersons well enough to know they weren't going to say anything stupid, even under questioning from Mike Wallace. If the producer was not being candid and there was more to his agenda for us, all the more reason we needed to deal with it head on. If all went well we might end up on the cutting room floor, but we would avoid those fateful words..."refused to comment on camera."

I obviously didn't do a good job convincing them. Even with the president of the company and the vice president of communications agreeing in principle that we should tell our story, the decision was made not to provide an on-camera spokesperson.

The segment that aired included an interview from jail of the subcontractor, comments from a "test pilot" and disgruntled former employee talking about the dangers of untested parts that might prove faulty, and from Congressman Dingell on the need for eternal vigilance on behalf of good over evil. In my opinion, there was not a clear enough distinction between the subcontractor and our company and the different roles each company played. I felt, for the first time, that we had been misled deliberately by a *60 Minutes* producer.

Chapter Four

I could argue that offering our own, high level spokesperson would have helped deal with this deception by letting us tell our own story more quotably than could be done in writing. I'm sure the media relations person saw the results differently as proof that he was right in advising caution and not sticking our neck out. In any case, Mike Wallace said the company declined to be interviewed. It wasn't as damning as some similar comments, but it didn't help our position.

Even more dangerous than either going on *60 Minutes* or saying no, is agreeing to an interview and then reneging. In 1990, Ed Bradley did a segment, produced by Robert G. Anderson, on General Development Corporation of Florida. The gist of the story was that the company quoted and charged different prices to buyers from outside the state of Florida than it did inside. On the program, Bradley said the company chairman "agreed to appear" on camera. Then the chairman, apparently being interviewed on a parking lot, was shown declining to answer questions "on advice of his attorneys." Bradley followed by asking the flustered executive for an "...apology. You can't answer questions, but why not apologize." No comment.

General Development Corporation was not our client, but four years later I met and worked with the man who had been in charge of public relations for them at the time of the infamous *60 Minutes* interview. He told the story, not much different than Ed Bradley described it on the air. The company felt that it could explain its pricing policies and the chairman agreed to an interview to take place in his office. Company executives worked to prepare the chairman. The PR executive was confident of the message and the spokesperson's ability

Saying No

to deliver it. The night before the scheduled interview, the company's attorneys decided the legal risks of what the chairman might say were too great and insisted the interview not take place. When the *60 Minutes* crew showed up for the interview, they were told the chairman wouldn't be available on advice of their attorneys. To no one's surprise except maybe the attorneys, Bradley and company didn't pack up and go back to New York. They waited on the parking lot until the chairman came out, then conducted their interview, with devastating results. General Development Corporation no longer exists.

Most damning of all is the classic picture we've all seen, of the person hurrying past the camera, perhaps with hand thrust toward the lens, sometimes with coat pulled in front of face. A man in upstate New York who had been shown on *60 Minutes* doing just that, filed a libel suit against CBS. He charged that *60 Minutes* had held him up to ridicule by "making him look foolish on national television." The judge's words were direct and to the point. Judgment was denied because, "*60 Minutes* did not make you look foolish on national television. They simply put you on national television making yourself look foolish."

47

Chapter Four

How to say no

- **Tell them why**. There must be a good reason for declining, so tell them the reason. It can't simply be fear. It shouldn't insult their integrity. If you can't think of a good way to explain why you're saying no, maybe you should reconsider that decision.

- **Help them find someone else.** *60 Minutes*, like all media, simply wants the best story. If you can suggest someone else who can help them achieve that goal, it helps get you off the hook gracefully.

- **Not taking part won't keep the show from running!** Companies often suggest that "if we don't take part they won't have any program." We have never known that to happen, that a story, if it was any kind of a story in the first place, wasn't done because one of the parties wouldn't appear.

Chapter Five

Fighting Back

Some companies have come to us after the fact, after *60 Minutes* has done a program on them, asking for help in damage control. One had been on the program but felt they hadn't come across well. One had declined to be interviewed, with the predictable result. In several instances, companies, or whole industries, had been scarred and wanted help in rehabilitating images or heading off further attacks.

Sometimes they ask how they can get *60 Minutes* to do a second program, in effect, how can they get a second chance. I'm not sure that's possible. I know we have never recommended it, even if it were possible. Our suggestion is that the best way to respond to *60 Minutes*, after the fact, is through other media outlets. If the point is to reach a similar audience, that can be done in other ways. If the issue covered on *60 Minutes*

Chapter Five

was important enough that it must be responded to, then it's probably an easy matter to get coverage on newscasts, especially local newscasts and in local newspapers, in markets that are most important. In some instances, we have alerted local TV stations and newspapers to the fact that the program is going to be on and is going to be of local interest so they can cover the broadcast as a news story. That usually gives the company involved a chance at another interview, a second chance to make the important points that may or may not get on *60 Minutes*.

Often the local media, particularly the local CBS TV station, will know in advance that *60 Minutes* is in town, working on a story. CBS uses local news resources, TV and newspaper, in its research, themselves contacting local media. This sometimes results in stories in advance of the *60 Minutes* program and certainly sets the stage for coverage after the fact. The *Rocky Mountain News* story that ran after the Coors program, became the basis for everything written later, including repetition of several factual errors in the report.

The point is, if the issue involved is important enough that the company feels it needs to respond beyond the *60 Minutes* broadcast, it should be approached as a whole campaign, using all available avenues to tell the story. We have mailed out the entire transcript of a *60 Minutes* interview *before* the program aired, getting our entire story into the hands of our key target audiences before it was subjected to the editor's knife. That was an offshoot of the idea of making a separate videotape of the complete interview, which I first heard of in the case of Illinois Power Company in 1979.

Illinois Power made its own videotape of the interview

between Harry Reasoner and its executive vice president, Bill Gerstner. The program aired on November 25, 1979 under the title "Who Pays? You Do...," produced by Paul Loewenwarter. Loewenwarter was the producer of the Harry Reasoner piece on unauthorized sale of videotapes featured in *60 Minutes'* own look at ambush journalism. This segment concerned the high cost of building a nuclear power plant in Illinois, with charges of cost overruns and mismanagement, all costs to be passed along to the customers of Illinois Power.

The company was displeased with the result, feeling that *60 Minutes* failed to convey facts they knew to be true about the company's side. They thought that Reasoner and his editors had deliberately distorted facts to prove a point on the program. Illinois Power's response was to produce what amounted to their own program in rebuttal. They hired a professional announcer to narrate it, with parts of what was aired on CBS followed by elaboration, either from the announcer or from footage of the interview that had not been aired.

"*60 Minutes'* Our Reply" was their title, opening over a shot of the familiar *60 Minutes* stop watch. The narrator said that, in addition to *60 Minutes* material, they would present what CBS "edited out, presented incorrectly, or chose to ignore." The narrator said, as if it were the ultimate indictment in itself, that their executive vice president had been interviewed for an hour and a half, from which only 2 1/2 minutes had been used on the air "to tell Illinois Power's side of the story."

Much of the IP rebuttal is done, not with unaired excerpts from the interview, but by the narrator. He takes issue with some of Reasoner's statements—the

Chapter Five

nuclear plant in question wasn't costing $30 million a month, as Reasoner said, only $22 million. The comments from Gerstner that were used on the program are strong, direct and to the point.

"The job is going very well. We're on schedule and on budget."

IP's detractors, mainly a handful of former employees, are represented by equally direct—and imminently quotable—comments.

"It's like Watergate..."

In other words, a fairly typical *60 Minutes* program.

The narrator corrects some factual errors, an apparent gross misstatement of the experience of the contractor building the nuclear plant and a statement that the staff of the Illinois Commerce Commission had submitted a report opposing IP's request for a rate hike. When tape of the Gerstner interview is used, showing what CBS "chose to ignore," even the most anti-media observer must begin to falter in unquestioned support of the company's argument. The outtakes the company submits as proof of the editor's bias are long, dull, and filled with jargon. It is easy to understand why the 14 minute segment didn't include Gerstner reading a long list of comparisons of percentage increases in the cost of nuclear power plants.

"That portion was never shown," intones the narrator. "Nor was comparison with other two-unit plants."

No kidding. *60 Minutes* didn't get to be the number one television program (actually, in those days, number two with more than 30 million viewers, according to the Wall Street Journal) by airing industrial films. When the narrator tries to clarify Reasoner's obvious misreading of a chart, the explanation comes across hopelessly

Fighting Back

garbled. Tape of Gerstner explaining why the chart might be interpreted to say something will be done in a week when in reality it takes several weeks, is even harder to understand, saying "the NRC (Nuclear Regulatory Commission) understands that." CBS "chose not to use" that long and confusing segment.

There were some things in the rebuttal that were damning to any impression of *60 Minutes'* objectivity. The company totally discredited the key witnesses on the other side, all disgruntled former employees with questionable credentials, even if they hadn't been fired for various degrees of incompetence. Worse, It was proved that CBS knew all about their shortcomings, including the fact that the main detractor had admitted lying about his educational credentials, including claiming a Ph.D. he never had. They had been presented on the program as experts in their field and their word presented as gospel.

Perhaps most disturbing was the fact that Harry Reasoner's one-line summations of key points, probably written by Loewenwarter, inevitably reflected a strong bias in one direction.

"A China syndrome of cost."

"The cost of building these plants has gone crazy."

Was the Illinois Power reply effective?

Sixteen years after the program, I am still asked about it by business people. Sometimes they mention it to refute some statement of mine about *60 Minutes* fairness or objectivity.

"Are you familiar with Illinois Power?" they ask, as if that represents axiomatic proof of CBS' bias and unfairness.

IP produced the reply tape to send to employees,

Chapter Five

customers, shareholders and the investment community, their important constituencies. According to the Wall Street Journal, requests for copies poured in from "everyone from university professors to major corporations to congressional leaders." More than 1300 copies were distributed in the months immediately following the broadcast. "Our Reply" became popular viewing at Rotary Clubs and other business forums. The tape itself began to be news, greatly leveraging coverage of IP's side of the story, and especially their message that CBS had treated them unfairly.

In June of 1980, seven months after the original broadcast, the Wall Street Journal ran a three column by ten inch story under the headline "Illinois Power Pans *60 Minutes.*" The tape, said Journal reporter Sandy Graham, "has focused new attention on news accuracy, particularly of powerful, hard-hitting TV news programs like *60 Minutes.*"

The Journal concludes, "even if future imitators of Illinois Power don't capture national attention the way the original did, their existence is expected at least to force reporters to look over their shoulders."

Clearly, then, "Our Reply " was a victory for Illinois Power. No one who has mentioned it to me in recent years could identify the site of the plant (Clinton, Illinois), say whether it was ever completed, or at what cost (I don't know either). All they know is *60 Minutes* treated Illinois Power unfairly and IP didn't take it lying down. They fought back.

As you may have surmised from my account of the reply, though, I view it a little differently. The Illinois Power tape is a textbook example of how *not* to get your message across on *60 Minutes.* The fact that their tape, in its finished, edited version ran 42 minutes tells the

Fighting Back

story. That's 28 minutes longer than the whole *60 Minutes* segment. If it takes a half hour to tell your story, you won't make it on *60 Minutes*. It took IP that long when the editing was under their control, and they didn't have to feel responsible for telling both sides of the story. Their own excerpts were long, confusing and boring. If *60 Minutes* hadn't been involved, no one would have bothered to watch the tape, even captive audiences; and I'm not sure those who watched did listen to, or understand, the message that was originally intended to answer Harry Reasoner's questions.

Dan Rather was quoted in 1981 in a media-watching magazine called *"Channels"*. "I plead for some perspective. When attention focuses on *our* mistakes, it's not whether Illinois Power did the job *they* should have done—it's whether *60 Minutes* did."

I agree with Rather. We can't control what they, the media do. We *can* control our part of the story.

Freedom Financial Corporation of Dallas, one company that came to us after the fact, seeking some measure of rehabilitation from a devastating *60 Minutes* piece. The segment was called "You're definitely a winner," Ed Bradley at his most incriminating, produced by Holly and Paul Fine. It involved the sale of time shares in condominiums and the use of enticing promises of prizes to get people to go look at the real estate involved. The company had declined to be interviewed, and Bradley's response on the air was another perfect example of the *60 Minutes* treatment of those who say no. Juxtaposed with interviews of young couples who thought they had won automobiles, but got knives or books instead, or who actually spent thousands of dollars for time shares they now decided

Chapter Five

they couldn't afford, Bradley said the company's president is "the type of Dallas businessman who might make J. R. Ewing proud." They showed pictures of his "million dollar house" in a ritzy neighborhood.

Then came the classic, closed-door picture, Bradley standing outside the office, company name on the closed door behind him.

"As you can imagine, we had a lot of questions to ask Bob Mead, but we were told on advice of his attorneys he wouldn't talk to *60 Minutes*. When his company pled guilty to conspiracy and two counts of mail fraud, they issued a press release, which pointed out that the investigation by the U. S. attorney's office found no irregularities in the sale of the time share units themselves."

The rest of the program, then, was an attack on those sales, featuring a former saleswoman who said she regularly lied to make sales. Other than her confessions of misleading statements concerning planned amenities, the worst criticism was that time shares were oversold and a customer's preferred week to use his or her share might not be available.

When representatives of Freedom Financial asked us for help after the fact, they gave us a tape of the *60 Minutes* program. Our first impression was that we couldn't possibly help them because they had absolutely nothing good to say. We told them, as we have told many over the years, "if you're really crooks, we can't make you look like good guys, and wouldn't even if we could." As usual, though, there were two sides to the story. Because of their own reluctance, their side had not been represented at all on *60 Minutes*.

Freedom responded by showing us the documentation *60 Minutes* had seen and used

Fighting Back

concerning the "prizes," plus information on other time share operations. They showed us a stack of letters from happy customers. Their objective was not to refute *60 Minutes* as much as to reach local media in various Texas areas where they did business, and to reach the Texas Legislature which was considering a bill controlling time shares. The Texas Attorney General had been prominently displayed on CBS. Freedom Financial's message was simple. We've cleaned up our act and want to work with the Legislature on these problems.

We told them frankly that we didn't see a lot to work with, but we spent two days helping them prepare for meetings with local media and with selected legislators. Some time later they sent us copies of a couple of resulting newspaper articles. A *Houston Chronicle* story quoted U. S. Attorney Bob Wortham as saying of Freedom Financial, after the court cases alluded to by *60 Minutes*, "their mailings are the cleanest in the industry." A Conroe, Texas newspaper quoted an assistant U. S. attorney, "Right now Freedom Financial appears to be doing exemplary work."

The Texas Senate and House passed revised versions of the proposed bill to regulate time sharing. The sponsor of the original, much harsher bill, said he was "disillusioned." He blamed lobbying by Freedom Financial for the changes.

That was the best we could do. Today, Bob Mead is the head of another company in a similar business and is a recognized leader in his industry. He is given a good deal of credit for pushing for passage of laws to curb the kind of abuses discussed on *60 Minutes*.

In 1981, another *60 Minutes* target fought back by

Chapter Five

releasing part of a tape of a *60 Minutes* interview, but this time it was not part of a company spokesperson's interview that had been left on the cutting room floor by CBS. It was a tape of what Mike Wallace said during a break in his questioning. Wallace was interviewing Richard Carlson, a vice president of the San Diego Federal Savings and Loan Association. The subject matter involved problems some customers had understanding contracts, causing some to default and lose their homes. Carlson, like Illinois Power, had his own videotape made. During that break to change tapes we've referred to before, Wallace commented on the complexity of the contracts. "You bet your ass they're hard to read, if you're reading them over the watermelon or the tacos."

CBS' camera was off, but the Association's wasn't. Wallace's comments, to his considerable embarrassment, found their way to other media. There were various half-hearted attempts to explain the remarks. Wallace's own explanation was probably the most accurate. He said he thought the remark might elicit some hint of Carlsons feelings toward the minority community.

We have always abided by a gentlemen's agreement when taping along with *60 Minutes*. It was unspoken at first, but since the San Diego incident, is usually expressed. That's an agreement that when the *60 Minutes* crew turns off its cameras, ours are turned off too. Seems fair, but our advice to Wallace is what we tell every potential interviewee: if you don't want to see it on TV, don't say it, whether you think the camera is on or not.

And then there is what corporate America seems to

Fighting Back

think is the ultimate threat to fight back. "If you use that, I'll sue!." In *Talking Back to the Media*, published in 1986, Peter Hannaford said *60 Minutes* had already been involved in 150 libel suits. I can't think, off the top of my head, of a single incidence of anyone winning a dramatic judgment against *60 Minutes*, although I obviously pay pretty close attention, I have to conclude that there hasn't been one. Hannaford cites what he appears to view as a moral victory, a suit filed against *60 Minutes* and Rather by a Los Angeles physician, Carl Galloway. *60 Minutes* alleged that Dr. Galloway had been involved in a scheme to defraud health insurance companies. He sued. According to Hannaford, Dan Rather testified on the witness stand that he had put in several calls to Dr. Galloway and they weren't returned. In his experience, Rather said, *failure to return his phone calls tended to prove suspicions of guilt.*

However much Dr. Galloway may have felt vindicated by that testimony, he didn't win a penny in damages. His lawyers couldn't prove the "actual malice" required to win a libel suit.

I can't help but think of Don Hewitt's words on his own program. "I have a feeling we shouldn't be trying to get people to talk to us who obviously don't want to talk. In fact, what you're asking a man to do is to testify against himself. You shouldn't do that."

You're right, Don. How does that square with the assumption that failure to return phone calls proves guilt?

Chapter Five

Tips on fighting back after *60 Minutes*

It's a lot tougher to fight back than to get your story told in the first place. We have still never found an instance where we didn't think it would have been easier to score points on *60 Minutes* than to try to recoup after the fact.

Consider responding through other media outlets. It's more important to respond to the issue, than to *60 Minutes*. If the issue is important, other outlets including print media, direct mail or advertising can be used to respond. If the response is really only to bruised ego, other means, perhaps internal, may be the way to go.

Either way, our story has to be interesting! As Illinois Power proved, no matter how good your argument is, it's a lot harder to get someone to listen if you make it deadly dull. *Don't preach, don't teach.* One reason being skewered by *60 Minutes* can be so deadly is that they know how to make people pay attention. We have to do that too.

The threat of a lawsuit doesn't scare anyone. That ultimate weapon of corporate lawyers, "if you say that we'll sue," usually only whets the appetite of any news medium. If your facts are strong enough to win a lawsuit, they ought to be strong enough to prove your point in the news. or to prove there is no story in the first place.

Chapter Six

The Stars

They call themselves "correspondents," although in the early days they were editors and co-editors. Never hosts. You'll often catch them referring to themselves simply as "reporters" for *60 Minutes*. That tells you a lot about the way they think and the way they approach their jobs. They are the stars. There are, in fact, no bigger stars in television, whether measured by the number of people who watch them, and have watched them for more than a quarter century, by the amount of money they make for their network, or by the number of imitators they have spawned. I think of Barbara Walters and Hugh Downs as hosts of *20/20*, and of Diane Sawyer and Sam Donaldson as hosts of *Prime Time Live*, but there are no hosts of *60 Minutes*.

Here's a quick quiz to determine your expertise on

Chapter Six

the subject.

How many "correspondents" have there been? (This doesn't count Andy Rooney.)
Who was the first?

How many have been women?

Which one was offered the job of press secretary to Richard Nixon?

I'll bet that, unless you've read Don Hewitt's book, *60 Minutes Minute by Minute*, that last one gotcha. Let's see about the others.

How many correspondents have their been? I count nine to 1996: Harry Reasoner, Mike Wallace, Morley Safer, Dan Rather, Ed Bradley, Diane Sawyer, Steve Kroft, Meredith Vieira and Leslie Stahl.

Who was first is a trick question. An argument could be made that Harry Reasoner was the first. Mike Wallace is the essence and the symbol of the program. His name and *60 Minutes* have become interchangeable when business executives talk about that dreaded time when *60 Minutes* or Mike Wallace might call. But in fact, the program was conceived with Harry Reasoner in mind as host, excuse me, as editor. Hewitt said he wanted a personal touch, quite different from the approach of the weighty news documentaries of the day. Reasoner, known for his light touch on CBS newscasts, fit that bill. But before the first program aired at 6:00 pm Eastern time on September 24, 1969, Mike Wallace had been added, so the real answer is that Harry Reasoner and Mike Wallace were both first. They would remain the anchors, in the true sense of the word, of *60*

The Stars

Minutes for two years until Reasoner was hired away by ABC for his ill-fated pairing with Barbara Walters.

There have been three woman correspondents. Yes, Diane Sawyer was the first. Lesley Stahl is the latest. Did you forget Meredith Vieira?

Can you imagine Mike Wallace as press secretary to President Nixon? How might the course of history have been changed! Hewitt said in his book that Nixon made the offer and that Wallace seriously considered it. For better or for worse, cooler heads prevailed. Yes, Diane Sawyer worked in the White House for a while before joining *60 Minutes*, but not as press secretary.

The correspondents are clearly the stars, and each has put his or her own stamp on the program, but the nature of the beast is such that they, like the interviewees, are mostly at the mercy of the producers. Jonathan Black said in *Channels* magazine, "given our addiction to heroes—a habit bred in the glamour gossip of *People* magazine and on the talk-show circuit it's inevitable perhaps that these on-screen stars should have become television's Four White Knights, indefatigable hounds of justice who pursue and nail the corrupt meat inspector, the Medicaid swindler, the mail-order minister. But, appearances not withstanding, our heroes often play walk-on roles in the weekly Sunday drama." The "Four White Knights" at the time that was written were Dan Rather, Harry Reasoner, Morley Safer and Mike Wallace.

Channels continued, "Once a story is 'blue sheeted'—given the go-ahead—it's the producer who hits the field, prepares the research, sets up interviews, and generally tailors a segment's focus. Then and only then, does the correspondent arrive on-scene to be

Chapter Six

briefed for the interview segment. This division of labor places the correspondent at a dangerous remove from a story's development. It also makes his interview less a flexible probe for information than a mock trial with the verdict already determined by the producer's pre-set questions. Moreover, the producer decides in most instances who should, and who should *not*, be interviewed. And that decision may be influenced by a segment's predetermined slant."

While that description is technically basically correct, I think it does a disservice to the correspondents. In our experience, they have more input into the early decision making process, including the go or no go decision, than this would reflect. It was Mike Wallace himself who called Coors to convince them to take part in that program. In another case, our client had several conversations with Leslie Stahl in weeks prior to an interview. So I believe it is unfair to depict the interviewers as simply reading questions handed them by the producer.

Nor do I agree that the verdict is "already determined by the producer's pre-set questions." Those pre-set questions, in the hands of Mike Wallace, turned the tables on the union rep in the Coors segment. The same was true of Wallace's handling of questions in a segment on Tyson Foods. Harry Reasoner's questions to two different oil company executives in the segment on leaking tanks led to two opposite conclusions or impressions. I believe it is ultimately the correspondent who determines the *denouement* of a segment during the interview, and then in the editing session with the producer and with the boss, Hewitt himself.

Sometimes more than one producer is working on a segment for the same correspondent at the same time.

The Stars

That can mean the correspondent is traveling and doing interviews on two (or more) stories simultaneously. We were working with a client to prepare for an interview with Leslie Stahl. We knew that the week before our interview was scheduled, she was in Hong Kong, flew back to the U. S. for a quickly scheduled interview with Hilary Clinton, then back to Hong Kong. We didn't expect her to be able to concentrate very much on our story that week. If anything, I think the pressures imposed by this system only prove how good the correspondents are at their trade.

Don't get the idea I'm saying they can always be trusted to be fair, forthright and even-handed. All those things people have complained about and sued for have happened. Prepare for the worst and hope for the best. The biggest impact of the correspondents, though, is in the personal imprint each one's style imparts to the program. These personal characteristics affect the kind of segments each is most likely to do, and how the interviewee will be treated.

Wallace is known for confrontation and gets confrontational segments. Safer, kidnapped from a job as CBS London Bureau chief to join *60 Minutes*, maintains his old world charm and renaissance approach. He is as capable of attack as any of them, but he is at his best when profiling the former East German orchestra conductor who now heads the New York Philharmonic or doing a fairly straight, if poignant, documentary on lost children of Argentina. Only Safer could make art thefts from a Boston museum fit on *60 Minutes*. Ed Bradley unabashedly loves show business, or at least the music business. His sensitive interview with Lena Horne is a classic, almost equaled by his segments on Aretha Franklin and Yehudi Menuhin.

Chapter Six

So, who is most likely to pull dirty tricks?

Our computer records aren't meant to be complete. We log programs at random. But they go back to 1982 and cover 14 pages of single spaced agate type. Those samples make it clear that the answer is all of them. Some of the best known ambushes involved lovable Harry Reasoner. During his tenure, Dan Rather may have been more feared than Wallace. Along with his sensitive profiles, Ed Bradley has logged an impressive list of what we catalog as dirty tricks. Ambush interview on a Florida parking lot. Hidden camera pictures in a Los Angeles parking garage. Ambush interview in another parking garage, ironically this one the ambush of a reporter for the *National Enquirer*. Several segments where Bradley pulls what we call the hidden memo, some surprise document, "I have here..." which the victim obviously hasn't been made aware of in advance. Hidden camera. Bradley holds what, as far as we know, is the record for dirty tricks in one program: hidden camera in van, hidden camera on person, *60 Minutes* employee posing under cover, hidden audio tape, on-camera ambush confrontation with tape— all in one program. In another segment, Bradley rather proudly says CBS set up a hidden camera, though it produced no footage used on the program. He pulled a surprise document on the same program. And he's logged several "they declined to be interviewed."

Those are actual quotes from our files of randomly taped *60 Minutes* programs. In fairness to Bradley, I must say we have a large number of comments as well that say of his segments, "very fair interview," "straight interview," "no tricks." Bradley does one other thing, a trait he shares with Lesley Stahl, that may prove most damaging of all to his victims. "Ed Bradley's technique of the incredulous question makes his points," our notes say. "You mean no one looked at this?" These questions are usually asked of the other side, not directly, so that the response to the incredulous question is simply yes or no and the indictment stands. Stahl's incredulity is more often expressed at the end of an answer, making her own feelings or judgment clear. In a piece on government pensions, after ambushing an outgoing U. S. Senator on a Washington sidewalk ("I have a feeling we shouldn't be trying to get people to talk to us who obviously don't want to talk."—Hewitt), Stahl talks about Gerald Ford's dual pensions for being President and from Congress. "No wonder he plays golf so much," she concludes. By snide comments, sometimes made in a studio after the interview, or by facial expressions, she lends her editorial comment to almost every answer in one of her interviews.

I was a great admirer of Lesley Stahl as a reporter and as White House correspondent. I think she fits the mold of a *60 Minutes* correspondent better than did Diane Sawyer or Meredith Vieira. But she is no less dangerous, from the point of view of those being interviewed, than any of her perhaps more notorious colleagues. And that's really the point. There is no safe haven. They're all equally tough and equally dangerous.

In our own, in-house, just for fun surveys, it has been interesting to note that each person remembers *60 Minutes* differently based on when they "tuned in." It seems to be easy to forget that Dan Rather was ever on *60 Minutes*, although he was there for five years. I suppose that's because he is so identified as anchor of the Evening News, but those who discovered the program in the 1976 to 1981 time period tend to think

Chapter Six

Rather was one of the originals. Some don't remember Diane Sawyer's stint, beginning in 1984, nor that of Meredith Vieira, who joined as a team with Steve Kroft.

When Reasoner left CBS for ABC, he was replaced by Morley Safer. Safer provided the needed contrast with Wallace, perhaps even more than Reasoner. Safer and Wallace *were 60 Minutes* for five years. For the 1976 season, the decision was made to expand to three correspondents and Dan Rather joined the group. Rather provided some of the most memorable confrontations, probably most famous, his meeting in a meat locker, surrounded by dangling carcasses, confronting a white coated inspector with a counterfeit stamp. I remember thinking many times, "Dan better watch it or he's going to get himself killed one of these days." He didn't of course, and stayed on to become part of *60 Minutes* first four-person team when Reasoner returned in 1979. Now it was Reasoner, Wallace, Safer and Rather.

How would you top that foursome? Hewitt had to try when Rather got an offer he couldn't refuse, to replace the legendary Walter Cronkite on the Evening News. He did it by hiring the program's first African-American correspondent, Ed Bradley. The first woman, Sawyer, came aboard three years later, in 1984. The first time a third person, Rather, was added to the team, there was some concern at CBS over how three people would find enough air time to share. When Reasoner returned, there were four. With the addition of Diane Sawyer, the program now had five correspondents, the number they've stayed with (with a few variations) since. Obviously they're not all on every program, since the typical *60 Minutes* is still divided into three stories, plus Andy Rooney. It speaks well of the spirit of the program

The Stars

that we have never been treated to public squabbles over who doesn't get enough air time.

In September, 1989, Fairchild/LeMaster published a newsletter to our clients with an item headlined, "Preparing for another year of *60 Minutes*." Here's part of what it said:

"The champion of news magazine programs goes into its 22nd year this fall with two new correspondents, Meredith Vieira and Steve Kroft, joining Mike Wallace, Harry Reasoner, Ed Bradley and Morley Safer. Vieira and Kroft come from CBS' *West 57th*, where they didn't necessarily strike terror in the hearts of those interviewed.

"Executive Producer Don Hewitt says they'll be worked into the program slowly. It is more likely that *60 Minutes* will put its stamp on them than vice versa. Don't expect any major changes in approach to stories or interviews."

Eight years later, a veteran of such *60 Minutes* programs as the one on which he asked presidential candidate Bill Clinton and his wife, Hilary, about charges of infidelity, Steve Kroft described his job to James Brady in "Parade" magazine:

"It's certainly the best reporting job in television, and it's what television jobs ought to be. TV has changed. People are rising to network anchor spots having done very little reporting. We (the *60 Minutes* crew) are all reporters and not anchors. We've all had long careers and have done stories all over the world."

The newsletter also said that our company had worked on three *60 Minutes* programs in the first half of 1989, bringing our total to nine, "which we will assume to be a record until proven otherwise." The record was never challenged, and the number reached 25 in 1997.

Chapter Six

The lead story in that newsletter was about another program on another network. Under a headline "Not Quite Ready for Prime Time," we welcomed a new ABC program hosted by Diane Sawyer and Sam Donaldson, *Prime Time Live.*

On paper, at least, *60 Minutes* had six corespondents for a brief period. In fact, Hewitt may already have known that Harry Reasoner was near death. I had seen Reasoner in April of 1989 as he interviewed one of our clients. Strange to say, it was the only time I have ever been in the room when the *60 Minutes* interview was taking place, the only time I have been face to face with one of the correspondents. Our job has to be done before the interview. Unlike the old gunfighters, we ride off into the sunset *before* the actual shooting starts, but it's not just to get out of the line of fire. Some of our clients are a little worried about how *60 Minutes* might respond if they saw one of us. Actually, they don't need to worry. I'm sure that, if I walked into a room with Mike Wallace, Morley Safer, and all the rest, they'd have no idea who I am. We do our job quietly, as low profile as possible. I doubted that anyone from *60 Minutes* would even recognize our name until recently when I was called by a public relations newsletter wanting an interview. The reporter said he was given our name by a senior producer for *60 Minutes.* Hmmmm.

It was Reasoner's 65th birthday, April 18, 1989. I was shocked when he walked into the office for the interview at how small he looked, how frail, how old. He was the same, pleasant Midwesterner that you always saw on TV, friendly and cordial to everyone in the room or that he met on his way to it. As the interview began, I was standing so that I could see a monitor with the TV

The Stars

picture and look beyond that to the real thing. I was stunned as the interview started to see the old Harry Reasoner on the screen. I don't mean the old one in years, but the same old Reasoner we had watched for years. Ten years had fallen away. The grayness I had seen on his face was gone. The voice was the same mellow, self-assured, and somehow reassuring voice I had first heard when I worked at NBC in 1967 and the pre-*60 Minutes* Reasoner was driving his CBS bosses nuts with his sense of humor.

I looked past the monitor. It was not just a trick of the camera. The live and in person Harry Reasoner had shed those years when the lights came on and he got his cue to begin. He was bigger, and younger, than life.

I'm glad I got to see him, once.

Chapter Six

Considering the stars

Some points to consider in deciding whether to be interviewed by *60 Minutes*:

There's no easy interview. Steve Kroft or Morley Safer are just as likely to ask tough questions as Mike Wallace.

Each does have a different style. In preparing for the interview, its important to consider that style, the pacing, the types of trick questions favored by each.

The public knows them and trusts them. No matter what you hear about how the public doesn't trust the media, remember they watch Mike and Morley and Ed every weekend. You won't win by getting into a fist fight with them. No one ever has.

Chapter Seven

The Producers and Their Dirty Tricks

Having tried, in the true spirit of the American star system, to make a case for the importance of the stars, now let me agree with Jonathan Black in *Channels* magazine. "Appearances notwithstanding, our heroes often play walk-on roles in the weekly Sunday drama. In fact, *60 Minutes* is largely the work of producers."

If you called Fairchild/Oppel today and said you had been contacted by *60 Minutes*, our first question would be, "who called?" Often that first call has been from a producer. If it was not, but was from an associate in the very preliminary stages of feeling out a story, we would suggest your first question the next time you talk to them should be, "who is the producer?"

Most people want to know who the correspondent will be. Is it going to be Mike Wallace? We can usually

Chapter Seven

answer that question by knowing the producer. They're generally assigned to one correspondent. If we know who the producer is, we can look back at a couple of recent efforts and determine who the reporter will be, as well as the style of the producer and the probability of dirty tricks. We can begin preparing a whole strategy from that simple piece of information, the name of the producer.

They may be less well known to the public than the stars, but there are producers who are no less legendary to us. Paul Loewenwarter, whose name appears often in these pages. Barry Lando, whom we considered Mike Wallace's personal producer. Marley Klaus, who holds our record for most dirty tricks in one segment. John Tiffin, who was Morley Safer's cameraman in London and came to *60 Minutes* as a condition of Safer taking the job. Lowell Bergman, who has been around for years and has the unusual distinction of working with three different correspondents. Robert G. Anderson, with Bradley, then Wallace. Josh Howard, with years of service for Wallace. Patti Hassler, with Safer and an occasional Reasoner. Anne deBoismilon, Reasoner to Wallace. Catherine Olian, Vieira to Stahl. Marti Galovic Palmer, mostly Safer.

It's dangerous to start any such list because of the inevitability of leaving off deserving names. Given the admitted limitations of our random sampling, though, these are the names that show up over and over, for better or for worse, as typical of *60 Minutes*. For the most part, I consider them giants of American journalism.

The first *60 Minutes* producer we worked with was Alan Maraynes, who produced the Coors segment. In a

The Producers and Their Dirty Tricks

newspaper interview after the program ran, he was asked something to the effect of, "when you went into the Coors brewery expecting the Coors brothers to wear black hats, weren't you disappointed when it didn't turn out that way?" Maraynes answered, "I don't know that we ever go in somewhere expecting somebody to wear a black hat. In fact, we don't care who wears the black hat and who wears the white one...as long as somebody does."

Those may not be Maraynes exact words, but let me quote Don Hewitt in his book. "The author cannot swear that all the quotes are verbatim, but he can swear that they're close enough not to be distorted, dishonest or disingenuous."

Close enough, and I believe importantly true of the thinking of most reporters and editors. We'd like somebody to be the bad guy, but we don't necessarily care whom. I think Maraynes had the answer to *Channels* magazine's charge that "the verdict" is "already determined by the producer's pre-set questions..." and that the segment has a "predetermined slant." The producers, like any reporters, have some pre-set guidelines, all right. The story has to be interesting, hopefully exciting, maybe surprising. It helps to have an identifiable bad guy. But it's not always business, and it doesn't always turn out to be who they thought it would be.

We have been burned by *60 Minutes* producers on a couple of occasions. For many years I told seminars that I had never been lied to by a *60 Minutes* producer, that they were generally very free and honest with information about what they were up to, because it would help us all put together our best efforts and that

Chapter Seven

would mean the best show. That changed with the defense contractor story covered in an earlier chapter.

The producer, Charles C. Thompson II, had been in discussion with the company's media relations manager who clearly got the impression that our company was a peripheral part of the story of a subcontractor that had been found guilty of faulty manufacturing and fraudulent testing of missile parts. I was not a party to those early conversations. I think it's possible that Thompson had underplayed our company's role early in the talks, thinking it would encourage us to take part. It had the opposite effect. The company spokesperson argued that, if we were a peripheral part of a bad story, we were better off *not* providing someone for an interview. I argued that the story, even as we knew it then, was important enough and potentially dangerous enough, that we should be the ones telling our side of the story.

After the company declined an interview, Thompson sent a scathing memo. Not only were we now not a small part of the story, but "prosecutors seriously considered indicting your company..., at the very least...was negligent..., your refusal to answer our questions...is evasive to say the least...I am forced to submit this list of questions in the hope that you might answer some or all of them."

There were twelve questions, couched in prosecutorial terms, but nothing the company couldn't answer or hadn't already answered. The implication of the three page letter, though, was clearly, if you don't do an interview, we can *make* you the focus of the story and you'll be the bad guy instead of the ones in jail. My words, not his. Thompson's letter concluded, "I wish you would reconsider your position and talk to us. If

The Producers and Their Dirty Tricks

not, I hope you will answer these questions in a speedy and timely manner. I believe that I have been very patient and fair in my dealings with you and your company. I may question your positions, but I don't question your right to take them."

I beg your pardon? I was stunned, after thirty years in the news business myself, at the arrogance of the letter. Again, Thompson may simply have thought he had tried the carrot and all that was left was the stick. Again, he had the opposite effect on the company than what he intended. He now gave credence to those who thought he planned a hatchet job all along. I still argued that, since we had good answers to all the questions, and since the bottom line was that someone else was at fault, was in jail, and we were ourselves victims, we should answer the questions on camera. The decision was no. The company provided written answers to the questions. The program didn't turn out badly, but it wasn't a victory, either.

I was troubled by the fact that Charles Thompson hadn't fit my conception of *60 Minutes* producers. I wondered, and still wonder, if it was because he had recently joined CBS after working for *20/20*. He was also based in Washington and specialized in covering the Pentagon, which in itself could make a newsman mistrust everyone. But we had to face the fact that there was a new source out there for future producers and perhaps reporters. The original batch came from CBS news or a similar network news background. Now, with programs like *20/20*, *Prime Time Live*, and, God help us, *Hard Copy*, *Inside Edition*, and others like them, there might be a new generation trained in a totally different way. We have never again assumed we wouldn't be lied to by a *60 Minutes* producer.

Chapter Seven

Producers sometimes conduct on-camera interviews themselves, as did Loewenwarter on the Illinois Power segment. Sometimes they are interviews of peripheral characters, leaving the major ones to the star. Sometimes the producer conducts a preliminary interview off camera, going over the same ground that will be covered by the correspondent later. For the segment on leaking gasoline tanks, Patti Hassler did a pre-interview interview that almost duplicated Reasoner's real one. Why? Because they really do want the guest's best shot, whether good guy or bad guy. This offers a good opportunity to practice and to look for anything that hasn't been anticipated, but don't for a minute think any potential "dirty tricks" will be disclosed in advance.

That's the second thing we look for once we know who the producer of a segment will be. First, it tells us who the likely interviewer will be. Second, it gives us a clue to how much we have to worry about dirty tricks (our term, of course, not theirs), and what kinds of tricks are their favorites. Then we can include in our preparation how to deal with those tricks if necessary. Rome Hartman liked the ambush, following a target along the sidewalk or showing up at a luncheon where a CEO who had declined to be interviewed was making a speech. Josh Howard was especially tough on those who decline to appear. David Rummel used slow motion, freeze frame shots of uncooperative witnesses, making them look especially guilty and caught in the act of something not quite defined. Chris Whipple used CBS employees posing as job seekers.

According to our files, the all time world champion of dirty tricks is Marley Klaus, a producer for Ed Bradley.

The Producers and Their Dirty Tricks

She first showed up in our dirty tricks file in 1989 with an Ed Bradley piece entitled, "Doing Business with City Hall." It was an expose´ of fraudulent minority contracts in Chicago. CBS set up a hidden camera which Bradley alluded to in the program, although it evidently produced no footage worth using. On the same segment, Bradley confronted a city official on camera with a document pulled from somewhere. "I will have to get back to you on that," the official said with a guilty look. It was a dirty tricks doubleheader, but it was only a faint promise of what Marley Klaus could really do.

"The Orange Juice Man" was a segment of *60 Minutes* on January 1, 1993. It was the story of migrant workers in Florida, exploited by the company store. The workers were shown in terrible living conditions where they were kept in virtual slavery because they were charged for every amenity and kept in constant debt to the company store. To get their material, Klaus and Bradley used a camera hidden in a van, just like in the spy movies. They had another camera hidden on a person so a conversation could be videotaped without one party knowing it. A *60 Minutes* employee went under cover as a worker, then audio taped a conversation with a Florida state official. That sounds like a grand slam, but it was topped when Bradley confronted the unsuspecting official on camera with the undercover tape. The CIA (or KGB) couldn't have done a more complete job, but even as I made notes cataloging the dirty tricks, I found myself applauding what CBS had accomplished in exposing the exploiters of migrant workers and the state officials who let it happen.

Don't assume that the public automatically disapproves of what I've called dirty tricks. I found myself personally applauding their use in Florida. I

Chapter Seven

applauded Dan Rather's catching the crooked meat inspector red handed. Most of us applaud when some government official or agency is found guilty of something, dirty tricks or not. In preparing for an interview, it's not enough for us to recognize the tricks and point them out or to complain about them. We have to avoid letting such tricks make us look guilty. That can be done with proper preparation. We check on the producer's propensity for tricks not as a guideline on whether to agree to an interview or not, but so we can prepare for them just in case.

Finally, knowing who the producer is can give us a glimpse of the probable subject and style of the program. Not all, but some producers lean heavily toward one kind of segment. A look at the long list of Morley Safer programs produced by John Tiffin shows their love for profiles of people and places. "Teddy Kollek of Jerusalem." "The Critic," about Frank Rich, chief drama critic of the *New York Times.* "Brezhnev's Daughter," portrait of the daughter of the late Soviet dictator, now a down-and-out alcoholic. "Stradivari," story of the violin. And yes, "The Muppets." That one ran twice, repeated when Muppeteer Jim Henson died.

Charles Thompson II is still likely to be working on something related to the Pentagon, and probably not favorable to the government or defense contractors. "USS Iowa," questioning the Navy's conclusions about an explosion on that ship. "Victims of Just Cause," alleging a U.S. coverup of civilian casualties in the invasion of Panama. "If Push Comes to Shove," alleging that faulty weapons would endanger U. S. troops in the Persian Gulf. Not all dirty tricks are as flagrant as the ambushes and hidden cameras. Our file on Thompson says of various segments he's produced, "well done, but one-sided...some erroneous conclusions left standing...heavily one-sided...".

Chapter Seven

What knowing the name of the producer tells us:

- who the interviewer will probably be

- what kinds of tricks might be used

- what kind of story it will probably be

Favorite 60 Minutes Dirty Tricks:

The ambush. Catching someone on camera when they don't expect it—most often on the street or in a parking lot.

The surprise document. A document, letter or memorandum produced as a surprise to the interviewee to elicit an immediate and unprepared comment.

The hidden camera. With modern technology, the camera can be hidden in a ball point pin.

The undercover agent. CBS employees have posed as job seekers, migrant workers, customers out shopping, usually in conjunction with other dirty tricks like the hidden camera or the ambush.

Chapter Eight

The Blues

Some of our clients have been contacted by *60 Minutes* several times on different subjects, but very few have actually been *interviewed* for the program more than once. One that has been is Blue Cross/Blue Shield Association. The first of the two interviews was the clearest of victories. The second, marginal to disappointing.

I had never directly worked with Duane Carlson, Blue Cross/Blue Shield's director of communications. I had done some convention seminars for them and that's how he knew to call us when *60 Minutes* called him in 1989. CBS's interest was prompted by a *Wall Street Journal* article in April under the headline, "Has Medicare paid out billions actually owed by private insurers?" A sub-headline said, "Blue Cross plans in Michigan and New York are cited so far in federal

Chapter Eight

inquiry." Both the *New York Times* and *Washington Post* had followed up on the *Journal* story. Now *60 Minutes* was working on a piece.

My conversation with Carlson was typical.

"Who's the producer?"

"I talked to Bob Lang, who says he's the producer. He says they want to talk to us as an intermediary."

Lang had told Carlson that another insurance company, named in the *Wall Street Journal* as under criminal charges, would be a prime source for the story. Carlson had also learned that Harry Reasoner would be the correspondent, and that Lang intended to complete his interviews in the next two weeks in the hope the program would air in early May, less than a month from the first contact.

"Great job," I told Carlson. "You've done most of my preliminary work for me."

I told him I was encouraged by the time table. Pushing for a quick air date often meant CBS was approaching a piece more as a news story than an in-depth documentary or expose´. Lang's name set off no bells or red lights in our computer. Carlson also knew from internal sources that CBS had already called Blue Cross/Blue Shield plans in Michigan and New York, so he felt there was no way the Blues could stay out of the story even if they wanted to. We agreed the best course was full speed ahead.

Duane R. Carlson joined Blue Cross/Blue Shield in 1966. Like many of the best of a couple of generations of corporate public relations people, he came from a background of print journalism. At 22 he was said to be the "youngest newspaper editor in America," as editor of a newspaper in Warrenville, Illinois. He edited a group of suburban newspapers and pulled a stint in corporate

PR for Montgomery Ward before joining McGraw Hill. He was editor of their *Modern Hospital* magazine (now *Modern Health Care*) when hired away by Blue Cross.

In addition to a background that suited him perfectly for his job, Carlson had something else going for him that is lacking in many corporate communications jobs today. He was truly in charge of communications for Blue Cross. His responsibilities included media relations, public relations, advertising, consumer affairs, graphic standards, publications (internal and external) and special events. The latter included matters as complicated as Blue Cross/Blue Shield's sponsorship of the Olympic games. He had a competent support staff in Chicago, where the association is headquartered, and in Washington, D. C., but he had hands-on knowledge of virtually everything happening involving the Blues. And he seemed to have the total confidence of Bernard Tresnowski, president of the association.

Carlson also seemed to have total confidence in himself. He was confident he could deal with *60 Minutes* as he had dealt with media for the association for 23 years. He also knew, though, that part of being good at what he did meant using all the tools available, so he called us, not as a cry of weakness, but as one more step in building a position of strength. In a three page memo to Tresnowski, he outlined the factors leading up to the *60 Minutes* inquiry, everything he had learned since about the thrust of the program, and our strategies so far. He concluded his memo:

"'I wanted you guys to be proactive, but this is ridiculous.'...Richard Nixon, memo to Gordon Liddy and John Erlichman."

I met Barney Tresnowski 24 hours before he met Harry Reasoner. I flew into Chicago from Dallas on

Chapter Eight

Tuesday morning to spend the afternoon getting ready for the next day's interview. Carlson and I went over the general strategy that we had discussed many times on the phone. We hoped to surprise them up front by agreeing to the problem, rather than denying it. Barney would, in fact, say the problem was a lot bigger in terms of possible dollars unaccounted for than the *Wall Street Journal* had indicated.

The key messages Carlson wanted to get across in the interview were: Blue Cross and Blue Shield plans have done an outstanding job in their role as Medicare contractors; if the government expects additional effort from Medicare contractors, it should be willing to fund them; Blue Cross and Blue Shield's partnership with the government on Medicare is one of the finest and longest-standing (23 years) public/private partnerships in the country; the most important area for improvement of the process would be to make sure providers and those over 65 know how important it is that private coverage be reported up front.

Those messages made up one page of a three-inch-thick ring binder Carlson gave Tresnowski to study. They were followed by 12 questions we expected to be asked, and the factual answers to those questions. One page of messages, 12 questions and their answers. The rest of the three inches of paper was background material on legislative and legal actions and Medicare in general. My job now was to help imbed the key messages in Barney's mind and rehearse him in giving the shortest, honest answers to the questions, then making his own points as they applied to the subject of the question.

We didn't use a camera in that practice session, as we usually did in preparing for *60 Minutes*. Because of the press of time—I would have less than four hours—we decided to concentrate on the messages and simply describe the physical setup Tresnowski would face. The interview would take place in a small conference room just outside his office. He would be seated at a table, on which he could place his notes. Reasoner would be across from him.

In the four hours available, I gave Tresnowski a quick course in handling the media, dealing with tough, sometimes trick questions, focusing on his messages. On a flip chart placed in the same conference room where Reasoner and his crew would set up the next day, Carlson and I drew three columns. On the right side, we put the messages we hoped would make the final editing cut; on the left, the toughest questions we expected from Reasoner. The middle column, considerably smaller than the other two, was labeled "answers." It was left blank, because, I explained, the answers had to be short and honest. We didn't want to spend an hour discussing the three-inch stack of material in Barney's notebook. He needed to know the basic answers, and to be confident that he had access to the answers. He couldn't avoid answering Reasoner's questions and maintain any credibility. But our efforts were directed at making sure those answers were followed by the points we wanted to make, in a quotable enough way to get on the air.

Once Tresnowski was comfortable with the messages, Duane Carlson and I began throwing questions at him, trying to anticipate the very order and manner in which Reasoner would ask them. Sometimes we suggested he shorten an answer that went on too long. Sometimes we honed the messages to make them more succinct and more quotable. Barney was

Chapter Eight

unflappable. At the end of our session, he and Carlson asked me to stay for the real thing the next day—the only time I have actually seen the *60 Minutes* taping live.

Those tales of terror striking the hearts of normal people when *60 Minutes* shows up in the lobby didn't hold true at the Blue Cross and Blue Shield offices in Chicago. The office staff greeted Reasoner as a star, everyone wishing him a happy sixty-fifth birthday. The crew set up just as we had expected, Reasoner across the table from where Tresnowski would be sitting, the single camera positioned just to reasoner's right, shooting past his shoulder at the Blue Cross president. I had suggested to Carlson that we not bring in a video camera of our own, but instead, to be unobtrusive and to save space in the little conference room, we would simply make an audio recording. Duane put a small tape recorder on a lamp table near the door between the conference room and Barney's office. He was positioned by the table. I stood in the doorway, as far out of the way as I could get.

I have described elsewhere how old, tired and ashen-gray Harry Reasoner looked until the camera came on and he shed ten years. That unmistakable midwestern voice began to ask the same questions Duane and I had asked the day before and Tresnowski fielded them deftly, never failing to make his own point. He seemed relaxed and confident and that confidence seemed to grow with each question and answer. The interview was only a few minutes old when Carlson's tape recorder stopped. He turned the tape over and tried again, but it was dead.

We agreed to a one hour interview, stipulating that Tresnowski had to end it at that point because of other

The Blues

commitments. Lang, the producer, said that would be fine. The CBS crew had to catch a plane for Miami for the next round of interviews on this story.

At exactly the half-hour mark, the cameraman announced he needed to change tape. During that short break, Lang conferred with Reasoner, going over their notes, obviously suggesting that the interviewer go back over some of the previous questions to elicit longer, or different, answers from Tresnowski.

For another half hour, Reasoner went over much of the same ground, with Barney repeating his answers, sometimes elaborating a little, sometimes giving different examples to prove his points. Having covered the ground we wanted covered, he was careful not to offer anything that might outshine the preferred quotes, careful not to compete with his own sound bites. As the allotted hour neared an end, Reasoner looked at his producer and said, "I think that's all I have." Lang nodded and the interview was over—but not the taping.

The cameraman shifted his position. Until now he had focused only on Tresnowski. Now he positioned himself for some shots of Reasoner, and of both.

"We have to get some 'cutaways,' " Harry said, "pieces that can be inserted when something is edited so it won't look choppy. Now, sometimes people are afraid when this happens that we're trying to trick you—get you to say something you shouldn't, so just to make sure you know this is not going to be used with sound, I'm going to say, 'four score and seven years ago, our fathers brought forth on this continent, a new nation...'"

he softly recited almost the whole "Gettysburg Address" before the cameraman announced he had enough "cutaways". I have since wished I had *that* on

Chapter Eight

tape. It occurred to me that Reasoner's statement that some people suspect a trick was testimony that *60 Minutes* was hearing the criticism of some of its tactics, and was trying, in some ways at least, to shed that image.

As Reasoner and Tresnowski stood, shook hands and exchanged pleasantries, the producer, Lang, came over to where Carlson and I were standing.

"I noticed that your tape recorder didn't work," he said. "Would you like us to send you a typed transcript of the interview?"

Needless to say, Carlson was quick to accept. Sure enough, the complete transcript arrived in just a few days. It confirmed what we had thought, that Barney had done a flawless job. We couldn't find anything in the transcript we thought would be damaging or embarrassing if it got on the air. On the other hand, he had said all the things he wanted to say. Whether those comments got on the air was now up to CBS. Their choices would depend to a large extent on what they got in other interviews. We knew that before coming to Chicago they had done some taping in Michigan and Reasoner had emphasized some of the questions about Michigan Blue Cross in his second go round of questions. They said they were on their way to Miami. We had no doubt that meant interviews with elderly Medicare patients and their doctors and probably state insurance regulators. It was out of our hands now.

One of the major complaints about *60 Minutes*, and in fact about news media generally, is that selective editing process. We hear over and over, "I did a great job for ten minutes...or an hour...and then they picked out that little part and made me look bad." If only the boss, or colleagues, or customers, whomever matters, could have seen the whole thing....

In this case, they could. Illinois Power had tried to get more of their story out after the fact, by distributing their own version on videotape. Thanks to a faulty tape recorder, we had a complete transcript already in hand. Tresnowski and Carlson made a highly unusual, maybe unique, decision. Rather than waiting to see what got on the air and then maybe using the transcript to prove something important had been left out, they decided to send the transcript immediately to all the members of the board of the Blue Cross and Blue Shield Association and to various other key people. They would all know, even before the program aired, that Barney had accomplished his goals in the interview.

The transcripts went out. Barney began to receive rave reviews from his colleagues, accompanied by sighs of relief from some who had warned against any encounter with *60 Minutes.* And we waited. Lang had promised to let Carlson know when a date had been set for the broadcast.

And we waited.

I called Carlson several times over a couple of months, asking if he had heard anything.

"Nope." He had called Lang more than once, only to be told no date had been set.

Finally, Carlson called me.

"Ken, I've got great news!"

To appreciate his reaction, you have to understand that I had never seen or heard Duane Carlson show real excitement. He was a bundle of nervous energy, but, not unlike Harry Reasoner, he spoke in flat midwestern tones that didn't betray any emotion behind the words. He wasn't kidding. I could tell he really meant he had great news.

Chapter Eight

"Well, tell me!"

"Lang just called. They've decided not to air the program at all. He said they just couldn't make a story out of it!"

"Hmmmm," was my response. "Well, congratulations."

"You don't sound as excited as I am," he said.

I realized how cold or disinterested my response must seem to him and I laughed.

"Sorry Duane. Of course that's great news. In fact you've got the best of all possible worlds. Everyone who has seen the transcript knows what a great job Barney did, and yet you don't have to run the risk of a negative story because you proved there wasn't one. That's a total victory for you. But you've got to understand, I'd rather the program had gone on and Barney had triumphed on the air. I would have had another "Coors" to brag about."

This time, he laughed.

"Okay, but if you don't mind, I like it better this way, and I'd just as soon it never happened again."

But it did.

Lessons of Blues one

Take the offensive. Blue Cross considered this a victory because it never got on the air, but even if this encounter were called a draw, what kept it from being a *negative* story was the consistently positive position of Barney Tresnowski. Blue Cross did not take the position CBS expected and offered, that of defending losses in the Medicare program. *They didn't fight the wrong battle.*

***60 Minutes*, like most media, wants everyone's best shot.** The producer's helpfulness, in offering information needed to prepare for the interview and in providing a transcript, indicate once again that they have no vested interest in making anyone look bad. They get their best program when all sides give good accounts of themselves. The absence of a strong other side, attacking Blue Cross, was probably as big a factor in killing the story as was the strength of the Blue Cross arguments.

By the mid-1980s, *60 Minutes* was beginning to feel public criticism. Harry Reasoner went out of his way to allay some of the concerns that were being expressed and the entire crew seemed intent on avoiding an overtly adversarial approach.

Chapter Eight

The right answer is the right answer is the right answer. Reasoner asked some questions several times, in only slightly different ways. Tresnowski stuck to his guns, offering no choice of answers to those questions.

Chapter Nine

Blues Two

The world of health-care changed dramatically in the early 1990s, and the world also changed for Blue Cross and Blue Shield. Soaring costs of medical care and concerns over the number of Americans who weren't covered by health insurance became a prime issue in the presidential race between George Bush and Bill Clinton. The Blue Cross plan in West Virginia closed its doors, the first (and still the only) time that a plan had failed. People who thought their health insurance was paid up found it wasn't so. The financial health of all the Blue Cross plans was put under a microscope by state insurance regulators and the media. As the political season warmed up, congress began talking about a national health-care program. Clinton began promising "health-care reform." A committee of the united states senate with the intimidating and highly

Chapter Nine

newsworthy name of "the permanent investigations subcommittee," headed by Georgia's powerful senator Sam Nunn, began hearings on the status of health insurance in America. Any such "investigation" would have to center upon Blue Cross because the name had been synonymous with health insurance for more than half a century.

When Bill Clinton unseated the Republican president, health-care reform became one of his showcase issues. It achieved an even higher profile when he designated the first lady, Hillary Rodham Clinton, to take the active lead in putting together the reform plan to be submitted to congress. While part of the insurance industry fought the whole concept of national reform and what was being called "managed care," Blue Cross and Blue Shield came out early in support of sweeping reforms within the framework of the existing system of health-care, which they said was the best in the world.

Barney Tresnowski, as president of the Blue Cross and Blue Shield national association, was naturally a central figure for media attention to all these elements. He was interviewed by Ed Bradley for a CBS program called "Street Stories." The topic was the failure of Blue Cross in West Virginia. He appeared on *Nightline*, frankly disclosing his own salary in a discussion of the cost of health insurance. He took part in an ABC Town Hall broadcast from Chicago that was one of the earliest in-depth programs on the overall reform issue. That night, one of the participants talked about 15 million Americans without health insurance. A few minutes later, someone else matter-of-factly cited the 25 million Americans without insurance. By the end of the evening, 35 million was the unchallenged figure. When

Blues Two

the Clinton plan finally died of starvation in Congress, the figure being used was 75 million. Washington was saying, with polls to confirm it, that the need for reform of the health-care system was the number one concern of the American people. Less than two years later the issue wouldn't make the top ten list, but in the meantime the relationships of doctors and hospitals and insurers and health-care providers of all kinds would be changed forever. HMOs and PPOs and CHPAs (pronounced "chip-uhs"), all forms of those managed care alliances that provide lists of doctors and hospitals acceptable to the programs, proliferated. Hospitals sold or merged or formed alliances with doctors and other hospitals.

The Nunn committee asked questions about various Blue Cross practices, some general among the state plans, some unique to individual states. Spending for promotion, like tickets to major sporting events. Salaries and travel of executives. Creation of for-profit subsidiaries by the not-for-profit Blues. The fact that Blue Cross was a non-profit organization, but in direct competition with large profit making insurance companies, put it in an awkward position in answering those questions. What was legal and acceptable for the competition sometimes sounded unacceptable for the Blues, who were judged by a different standard.

The headquarters of Blue Cross and Blue Shield stayed in Chicago, but the emphasis of public affairs and government relations shifted heavily to Washington. Duane Carlson's Washington staff grew and took over more and more of the public relations and media duties. Whether because he was so embattled or because his influence was slipping away or simply because he was able, Carlson retired. His successor would office in

Chapter Nine

Washington.

Clay Mickel had been hired to head public affairs efforts in the nation's capital as part of the expansion of that office. He assumed the national role when Carlson retired, but it was made clear that he was acting in a temporary capacity until a permanent successor could be named. He was told he was considered a candidate for the job, but had to compete for it. Mickel had dealt with the Nunn committee and all the issues of the reform debate, but it was easy to see that the association was looking for something, or someone, else. The officers and board members who made the decisions felt the emphasis needed to be on political experience or influence. Mickel resigned to take a good job with a related health-care association.

His replacement came from among the number of recently unemployed members of the Bush administration. Alixe Glen had extensive experience dealing with national media. She was intelligent, capable and cool under fire. She was plunged into the national debate over health-care reform, congressional attention exemplified by the continuing Nunn committee hearings, and in early 1994, the renewed attention of *60 Minutes*.

The producer was Howard Rosenberg. The correspondent would be Lesley Stahl. I was an admirer of Stahl's work as White House correspondent, and when she was brought to *60 Minutes* I thought she would be a perfect fit, but I hadn't worked with clients on any of her segments. Alixe, from her own White House experience, knew Stahl well enough to call her directly and talk about the goals of the proposed interview with Barney Tresnowski.

Blues Two

There were adversarial tones to the discussions from the start and Glen warned about that in a memo to key people at Blue Cross. Several conversations with Rosenberg and with Stahl added to that perception. The issues would be all those that had been in the news for a year or more, obviously the Nunn committee agenda—spending by some Blue Cross plans the senator thought was excessive, advertising and promotion practices that were normal for businesses, but which looked different in the case of what was viewed by many as a public utility.

Blue Cross, and Tresnowski himself, had answered those questions many times, and were preparing to answer them before the Nunn committee in the near future. While there had been some flagrant errors at some state plans, most of the issues came right back to the question of whether Blue Cross and Blue Shield would be held to different and much higher standards than the companies with which they were more and more in competition.

Preparation for the Stahl interview followed much the same pattern as that of the earlier Blue Cross *60 Minutes* interview, but there were some differences. As far as I could tell, communication between Glen and Rosenberg involved considerable mutual mistrust. Stahl was only sporadically available for consultation, not unusual for a busy *60 Minutes* correspondent. The week before the Blue Cross interview was to take place, she was in Hong Kong working on one story, returned to the U.S. for an interview with Hilary Clinton, then back to Asia. We were concerned about her ability to prepare properly for our interview. And there was another difference. Glen and her staff prepared a briefing book for Tresnowski that was almost identical to the one

99

Chapter Nine

Carlson had prepared, except that the Q and A section that had been two pages long, this time ran to 22 pages.

As before, we went through a four hour rehearsal. Tresnowski answered all my questions smoothly and made our positive points. Essentially our goal was simply to explain that Blue Cross Blue Shield was a business, in a highly competitive field, and that most of the questions involved honest competitive practices.

I wasn't present for the actual interview the day after our rehearsal. When Alixe Glen called me after it was over, she gave it mixed reviews. Barney had done well, she said, in the first half of the interview, but got a little too argumentive in the second half. She said the interview had lasted two hours. I considered that very disturbing news. She also said there were several answers that had been factually wrong. Since the interview, she and her staff had contacted Rosenberg and Stahl to tell them some of the facts had been wrong, and to provide them with accurate information.

This time Glen had the interview videotaped and quickly produced our own written transcript. There were very few surprises. Much of the first half of the interview consisted of attempts to define Blue Cross, including its not-for-profit status. Stahl commented the Blues were, and should be, held to a higher standard than other insurance companies. She asked about the tax benefits of being not-for-profit. At one point Tresnowski explained, "Blue Cross Blue Shield plans, though they are not for profit, are neither charitable institutions, nor are they tax exempt institutions."

At another point, he said, in discussing the origin and evolution of Blue Cross, "but non-profit doesn't mean you don't make a profit. It means that you just don't give money to stockholders."

Blues Two

Another exchange went this way:

Stahl: "...just saying you're not-for-profit is very misleading, because you are for profit."

Tresnowski: "Well, we're not for profit. No we're not for profit."

Stahl: "But you make a profit."

Tresnowski: "We do make a profit."

Stahl: "Well, that's why it's misleading."

Tresnowski: "No it's not...let me explain that to you. A for-profit company, one that goes into the marketplace, sells stock, and, therefore, you're beholden to the stockholder. A not-for-profit company can make a profit, but it takes the profits and puts it into its reserve position. That's the distinction."

Confusing at best, that discussion that covered several typewritten pages of the transcript, might not have been damaging had it not followed questions about specific tax breaks Stahl said were enjoyed by the Blues. Tresnowski explained that most of the breaks they once enjoyed hadn't existed since 1987, but there was still one section of the U. S. tax code that provided a special deduction in some specific cases.

Stahl asked, "but you're saying by now, with these plans having changed over a while ago, none of them are taking this tax break?"

Tresnowski: "Well, I can't say none of them, some

Chapter Nine

of them probably continue to do so...but the vast majority of them are full taxpayers today."

He firmly believed that to be true. It wasn't. That was one of the errors Glen had corrected after the interview, sending a complete list of the plans and their tax status to CBS.

The second half of the interview covered the old familiar ground of plans that had been in financial trouble or trouble with regulators, of executive salaries and such expenditures as flights on the Concord and sky boxes at baseball games. Stahl asked about expenses for meetings at several places she labeled "resorts." Tresnowski explained that the association executives, dealing with 69 plans around the country, were constantly traveling and that they got special rates at many of those hotels.

Stahl:	"Then they're not golf weekends?"
Tresnowski:	"Oh no. We don't engage in those sorts of things."
Stahl:	"Really?"
Tresnowski:	"No."
Stahl:	"You had a meeting just last fall at the Scottsdale Princess hotel."
Tresnowski:	"No we didn't. We've never had a meeting at the Scottsdale Princess hotel."

The transcript indicates there was an "indecipherable" conversation among the CBS personnel, probably Stahl and Rosenberg.

Blues Two

Stahl: "You were a featured speaker at the conference. Had a dinner on October 19th. You spent $54,000 on food, a liquor bill of $8,000, and a reception a couple of nights earlier for another $7,000 liquor bill."

Tresnowski: "I'm not familiar with any of that. I don't even remember being at the Scottsdale princess."

Stahl. "You'd have to. It was just last fall in October."

My feelings of trepidation grew when I read that exchange. It was, in my opinion, a classic example of fighting the wrong battle. It also was just one of many instances toward the end of the interview that seemed to show Barney getting testy and argumentive. At least the issues were relatively unimportant, I thought.

Wrong.

There was also a general air about the interview, again, judging only from the written transcript, that bothered me. Howard Rosenberg sometimes interrupted with his own questions. Even though, as we have seen, producers play an extremely important role in developing the questions, and sometimes even do whole interviews, it's very rare in my experience for the producer to take such an active part when one of the correspondents is doing the interview. There were several times when Stahl and Rosenberg would interrupt the interview for discussion between themselves, Stahl trying to clarify something or Rosenberg trying to point her in a different direction.

At the conclusion of the interview, while the tape was

103

Chapter Nine

still rolling, Stahl, Tresnowski and Alixe Glen carried on a conversation that indicated Glen's fear that several points had been left unclarified that could give a very wrong impression.

Stahl: "Anything that I asked you that you haven't said isn't true, we've triple checked it. Talk to Alixe. And I'll call you if we're still confused, all right?"
Tresnowski: "Okay."
Stahl: "All right, I don't want to be wrong. I really don't want to be wrong."
Tresnowski: "Good."

The segment that actually aired on CBS focused on questionable business practices that Stahl said involved "fraud and abuse." As expected, Senator Nunn played a starring role, going down the list with Stahl. Tresnowski's responses made his points—that each plan was autonomous within guidelines set by the association, and while he didn't condone some of the more extravagant practices or expenses, they were not illegal or unlike practices within the industry. The difference, then, came down to the question of being not-for-profit and those tax breaks.

"When you're in business, you ought to be for-profit," Nunn said. "You ought to have shareholders. You ought to have accountability with shareholders, you ought to show the bottom line, and you ought to be a business."

I don't know whether anyone at Blue Cross expected that from Nunn, but I certainly didn't. I thought that was a stunning statement, that there should be no such thing as a not-for-profit business, especially when

Blues Two

referring to the health-care field where so many hospitals are proudly not-for-profit. Here was Blue Cross Blue Shield now being assailed for the very thing that had made them the symbol of community service over the years. Confusing as the term may be to explain, not-for-profit meant turning what was being called profits, income over expenditures, back into the plans instead of distributing the money to shareholders. Here was a powerful United States senator saying it would have been all right, even preferable, if Blue Cross had been distributing all that money as profits instead of spending it to be competitive in the industry.

In my opinion, it would have been a ridiculous argument and not at all embarrassing to Blue Cross—except for the tax breaks.

The pages-long discussion between Stahl and Tresnowski about tax breaks in the interview was represented in the program by two questions and answers.

Stahl: "I thought Blue Cross got a special tax break. Is that true?"
Tresnowski: "No it's not."
Stahl: "You get no tax breaks."
Tresnowski: "No."

In narration over pictures of the Blue Cross and Blue Shield symbols, Stahl said, "that's not true." Then the Texas insurance commissioner was seen saying "they still are being treated like the old Blue Cross Blue Shield they used to be."

Clearly, the implication was that Blue Cross Blue Shield was still totally tax exempt. Stahl then cited the specific part of the tax code that Tresnowski had told her left an exemption under certain circumstances, not

Chapter Nine

mentioning that the information came from him in the same interview. She said that *60 Minutes* called "every one of the 69 plans," and asked about tax breaks.

"Most of them," Stahl said, "referred us back to the association. Tresnowski, speaking for the plans, continued to play down the tax issue."

Cutting back to the interview, Stahl is heard saying "none of them is taking this tax break."

> Tresnowski: "Well, I can't say none of them. Some of them probably continue to do so because they haven't changed their business practices. But the vast majority of them are full taxpayers today."

Stahl jumped on that comment, quoting IRS reports that "in a recent year, 45 companies..." took the exemption. "A vast *minority*," she said.

This segment and some of the parts to follow, represent my worst experience in more than 15 years of dueling with *60 Minutes*; worst from the standpoint of what was being done to my client and worst from the standpoint of what everyone fears *60 Minutes* will do in the editing process.

When Stahl alluded to calls to the plans that referred CBS "back" to the association, then said Tresnowski "continued" to play down the issue, could there be any other interpretation than that they had gone back to Tresnowski for a second interview and that he continued to misrepresent the facts? That was simply not true. Tresnowski was interviewed only once and his comments were matched up with what CBS later learned. And where had they learned those facts? Calls

Blues Two

to the plans and IRS reports notwithstanding, that information was also part of what Alixe Glen, on behalf of Barney Tresnowski, had sent to CBS immediately after the interview. Tresnowski had been wrong. He told CBS he had been wrong. He sent correct information. But on the air he was represented as "continuing" to repeat misinformation.

In my opinion, *60 Minutes* went out of its way to make it appear Tresnowski was deliberately lying, when they knew that was not the case. The rest of the program strengthened that opinion.

The exchange over whether the association ever had a meeting at the Scottsdale Princess hotel was briefly touched, with Tresnowski saying "no, we didn't. We've never had a meeting at the Scottsdale Princess."

Again in voice over, added long after the interview, Stahl said, "Well, here's a reminder. The Arizona plan sponsored a conference at the Scottsdale Princess. Tresnowski checked in on October 18th and checked out on October 21st..."

It makes for great television by today's "investigative" standards, but there are a couple of problems. Tresnowski was asked about meetings of the Blue Cross Blue Shield *association* and answered truthfully. By the time the program aired, Stahl said, "the Arizona plan sponsored a conference..." where Tresnowski was the guest speaker. Again, he was made to look as if he was lying when in fact he was not. Would his response have been different if he had been asked about a meeting of the Arizona plan? Maybe or maybe not, but he was right when he said the association, the national organization made up of all-three plans, had not held such a meeting. He may have gone too far when he didn't

Chapter Nine

remember ever being at the Scottsdale Princess, even though that was obviously true also.

And again, the correct information was given to CBS by Alixe Glen immediately after the interview. When we saw the transcript, we recognized that Stahl was probably talking about that meeting of the Arizona plan. I had been on the same program with Barney. Well before the interview aired, *60 Minutes* knew the facts and chose to let the misstatements stand.

Remember the line in the interview about golf outings? It seemed innocuous at the time. Stahl was asking about that list of hotels and then added one line, "so they're not golf weekends?"

"Oh, no," said Tresnowski, "we don't engage in those sorts of things."

After that exchange on the final program, over a shot of golfers teeing off, Stahl said sarcastically, "That must have been some other Tresnowski who joined a gaggle of Blue Cross executives on the Las Colinas golf course last June..."

Then she showed, as if it were the ultimate smoking gun, a pro shop record of Tresnowski's tee time, "minutes after an association board meeting ended."

Again, the implication that Tresnowski had been lying, but of course he had not been asked, "do you ever play golf at these meetings?" The question, or rather the statement, slipped in at the end of a list of hotels, was "so they're not golf weekends?" To which the honest answer was, no.

I don't know why *60 Minutes* decided to make the issue one of Barney Tresnowski's credibility. They had plenty of legitimate material, important questions in the health-care debate. They had both sides covered. Why go out of the way to make it *appear* that Barney Tresnowski was lying? He was not, and when he had been mistaken, he had seen to it that *60 Minutes* got the correct information well before the program ran. No mention was made of that.

Barney Tresnowski is a decent, honest man. Whenever I think of him, I remember Leslie Stahl's words at the end of the interview tape.

"All right, I don't want to be wrong. I really don't want to be wrong."

Chapter Nine

Lessons of Blues Two

More is not necessarily better. There is always the temptation to believe that the more we are able to explain our position, the more likely the interviewer and then the editor will understand. Actually, since our goal is to *limit* the editor's choices, that's just not true. Most of the questionable parts of this interview came in the second hour. We suggest setting a definite time limit for any interview.

Stick with the game plan. No matter how well the interview is going, resist the temptation to tackle new issues or give glib answers to questions that have already been handled. The right answer is the right answer no matter how many times the reporter asks the same question.

Don't fight the wrong battle. It didn't really matter whether Blue Cross had ever had a meeting in Scottsdale. No good could come from arguing the point.

Avoid an adversarial relationship, before and during the interview. Mark Twain was right when he said, "Never get into a fight with a man who buys his ink by the barrel." You will not win a battle of intimidation with any reporter or editor, and certainly not with *60 Minutes*.

Chapter Ten

The Clones

There were other long-form news programs in existence when *60 Minutes* was created. There were the prestige Sunday public affairs shows, *Meet the Press*, *Face the Nation*, and the like. They mostly featured live interviews with one or two newsmakers, just as they do today. They were news interviews, not "news magazines" like *60 Minutes*. The new magazine was more akin to the old "documentaries" that CBS did so well, half hour- or hour-long "investigative" pieces covering a story in much more depth than was possible on a regular news program. Documentaries were the classical music or the art movies of television. Critics acclaimed them, networks won awards for them, the public generally ignored them. Don Hewitt produced documentaries before he came up with the idea for *60 Minutes*. He called them snoozers. Hewitt says his

Chapter Ten

formula for the new genre was simply to put three topics into an hour instead of one, and to let the correspondents demonstrate their personalities. Hardly the formula for MTV today, but a revolution for 1967.

In retrospect, it's surprising that it took so long for others to copy the format that became the most watched news program ever, and one of the most watched TV shows, period. Remember, though, that news programs had never produced good ratings. Not until 1996, with *60 Minutes* just short of thirty years old, did another network try to contest the time slot with a similar program. By then, every network had its *60 Minutes* clone.

One of the first, and one of the best, was ABC's *20/20*. While the selection and presentation of stories was very similar to that of *60 Minutes*, the ABC version used veterans Hugh Downs and Barbara Walters mostly as in-studio anchors. Walters and Downs sometimes did their own stories, but usually the correspondent would be a Tom Jarriel or John Stossel. *20/20* was surprisingly successful, although it would be several years before it's ratings began to rival *60 Minutes*. For its week-night time slot, where all other news programs or documentaries had failed to draw audiences, *20/20* proved highly competitive.

ABC debuted its second entry in the magazine wars in 1989. In a newsletter to clients, under the headline "Not Quite Ready for Prime Time," we reviewed the new program this way:

"We've seen enough of the new Sam Donaldson-Diane Sawyer program *Prime Time Live* to alert our clients to the potential dangers of taking part in the program. In some ways it combines the worst instincts of *60 Minutes* and the Morton Downey show. (At that time Morton Downey, Jr., was doing a talk show noted for his insults to his guests.)

"They like 'investigative' pieces using all the ambush techniques—hidden cameras, surprise interviews. Guests who accept the invitation to be present in the studio to answer questions aren't treated any more kindly than those confronted in the field. Expect to be blindsided and don't expect much logic in the line of questioning...

"Donaldson's stand-up comic routine directed at the studio audience is the part that reminds of Morton Downey.

"Fairchild/LeMaster is *not* advising clients to stay away from *Prime Time Live* altogether, although it's hard at this point to see much advantage to being on the program. We are not yet ready to add it to *Giraldo* and the Downey show as the only programs we have ever simply said don't do."

We offered these "guidelines" for anyone getting ready to go on "Prime Time":
* Be prepared and stick to the game plan, as with any media appearance.
* Expect the worst question possible. This is show biz and Diane and Sam make no pretense of taste or politeness in handling guests.
* Don't dignify Sam's one-liners to the studio audience. The most useful line for a *Prime Time Live* guest may well prove to be, "ah, come on Sam." That fairly well sums up our reaction to the show.

The powers at ABC apparently recognized some of

Chapter Ten

the same faults. The "live" part of the program, including the studio audience, soon disappeared. Donaldson was moved to Washington, leaving Sawyer in New York and the "Prime Time" format, other than the fact that Downs and Walters continued to share the same desk, became virtually impossible to distinguish from that of *20/20*.

CBS tried to clone its own success. *57th Street* was supposed to be a younger, hipper, *60 Minutes*, but failed to attract an audience. Then came *48 Hours*, hosted by *60 Minutes* alumnus and evening news anchor Dan Rather. It was slow to catch on and underwent changes from the original concept of following one story for, as the name would indicate, *48 Hours*. Rather played little part, other than narrating or introducing the segments. Unlike the quick abandonment of *57th Street*, the network stuck with the program, though, and the patience began to pay off in the 90s as news magazines began to dominate the network ratings. Another CBS effort, *Street Stories*, with Ed Bradley as host and correspondent, fared less well and came and went relatively unnoticed. *Eye to Eye With Connie Chung* came and went in a blaze of publicity over a controversial interview with the mother of Republican Congressman Newt Gengrich and internal disagreements between Chung and her evening news co-anchor, Rather.

NBC tried a program with the unfortunate title of *Expose´*. As syndicated programs began to crop up shamelessly copying the formats of the "super market tabloids," and as "tabloid journalism" became a phrase to compare their practices with the less savory forms of print journalism like the *National Enquirer*, the name *Expose´* didn't seem to fit a program hosted by the network's own evening news anchor, Tom Brokaw. After

The Clones

less than two seasons, *Expose'* went the way of *57th Street* and *Street Stories*.

Rather than abandon the field to CBS and ABC, NBC pulled out all the stops. Successor to *Expose'* was *Dateline*, one of its hosts, Jane Pauley, respected former host of the network's *Today* show. *Dateline* had a slicker, less frantic look than its predecessor. It gained respectability in spite of some problems like the infamous program in which NBC admitted using footage of exploding pickup trucks in which the explosives had been planted to produce the film. As with *48 Hours*, *Dateline* was given time to establish an audience. The results were such that NBC expanded the program to two nights a week, then three, then four. Finally, in 1996, *Dateline* became the first to challenge *60 Minutes* on its own turf, Sunday night.

Competitors and some critics had been expecting *60 Minutes* to fade for some time. All network programming was losing audience to cable, especially network evening newscasts. Where once the three had fought over how they divided some 50 per cent of the television audience, by 1990 they had seen that number drop to less than 30 per cent, then less than 20. *60 Minutes* numbers dropped too, but the venerable program stayed among the top ten and now commanded as big an audience as all three evening newscasts combined. The correspondents whose names were synonymous with the program were aging. Then came what many thought would be the final blow. CBS lost the mainstay of its Sunday programming. In one of the most dramatic switches in network history, the upstart Fox network outbid CBS for NFL football. *60 Minutes* lost its powerful

115

Chapter Ten

lead in.

Amazingly, the news magazine stayed in the top ten. It seldom came in first as it had in many past years, but it was still one of CBS' top performers, often the only CBS program in the top ten. The total audience continued to decline, though, along with the audience for all network programming. It seemed at times as if *60 Minutes* was trying to contribute to its own demise. An internal dispute over a segment on the tobacco industry turned into public accusations of censorship by the correspondents and Andy Rooney. CBS brass at the highest level evidently ordered Hewitt not to run the segment. It was broadcast much later, after the airing of a clothesline full of dirty linen. *60 Minutes* stayed strong, but the competition was getting fierce. The end result was that several competitors also began to show up in the top ten. Instead of *60 Minutes* dying, the news magazine genre became the hottest thing on network television.

In 1995, Ed Bark, TV columnist for the *Dallas Morning News*, wrote a column that was headlined "news mags are TV's hot properties." He began by mentioning two new entries in the race, both of which would soon disappear. One was Chung's *Eye to Eye*, the other a Fox program called *Front Line*, with Ron Reagan, son of the former president, as one of five correspondents. More significant was Bark's comment that "a night won't go by without at least one helping from this suddenly essential food group.

"Sunday is still home to CBS' *60 Minutes.*

"Monday brings ABC's Day One.

"If it's Tuesday, this must be *Dateline NBC.*

"Wednesday gotcha stumped? It's *48 Hours* on CBS.

The Clones

"Thursday's now a two-bagger; Connie and ABC's *Prime Time Live*.

"It wouldn't be Friday without ABC's *20/20*, now would it?

"And Fox's *Front Page* will be closing out the week..."

Bark pointed out that, of 92 network programs airing in prime time, no news show placed lower than 28th. "In order of finish, we're talking *60 Minutes*, *48 Hours*, (Katie) Couric's one-hour interview with First Lady Hilary Rodham Clinton, *20/20*, *Dateline NBC*, *Prime Time Live* and *Day One*. Even though it trailed the field, *Day One* drew more than three times the audience for show no. 92, Fox's Parker Lewis."

A quarter of a century after it's birth, *60 Minutes* had spawned a whole industry, one that might well prolong the life of the dying television networks. By 1995, *20/20* and *Prime Time Live* made regular excursions into the rarified air of the top ten, sometimes one, sometimes the other, even surpassing *60 Minutes*.

Dateline began to perform well enough that NBC added Wednesday and Friday versions. Other programs shuffled time periods, *Prime Time Live* moved to Wednesday, *48 Hours* to Thursday, but, except for Saturday, it was still possible to say, as Bark had said, that a night couldn't go by without at least one news magazine. By mid '96 it was not unusual for four or even all five of those programs to finish in the top ten or close to it. Most often, *60 Minutes*, broadcast on the night of heaviest TV viewing, still led the pack. NBC decided the time was right to challenge the champion on its home turf. In march, 1996, *Dateline* added a Sunday night version head-to-head with *60*.

Hewitt and the rest of the brass at CBS were not

Chapter Ten

unaware of the assault on their position. They had already announced some changes, such as eliminating summer reruns in favor of new programming. The week before *Dateline NBC*'s Sunday debut, CBS increased its advance promotion. Howard Rosenberg, *Los Angeles Times* television critic, headlined his review, "Hey, NBC! That hour belongs to *60 Minutes*."

"Like trick birthday candles that can't be extinguished, *60 Minutes* keeps glowing and glowing, while its competitors keep blowing and blowing.

"You'd think there would be some chivalry among old foes, that NBC, for example, would be so contentedly fat with its own epic success in the Nielsens that it would magnanimously sit back and pay homage to an enemy's greatness—by no longer challenging the longtime supremacy of 28-year-old *60 Minutes* on Sunday nights.

"After all, even while floundering on Sundays, NBC has continued to roll in profits due to its remarkable success elsewhere in prime time. So it could well afford to do the honorable, gallant, romantically old-world thing and mercifully keep hands of this relatively tiny fiefdom of success on lowly CBS.

"But nooooooo!

"There are no respectful tips of the lance in television warfare, which makes the Balkans look like Switzerland. Being third or even second is never good enough. Coexisting is never good enough. The siege never ends. No matter the circumstances, the goal is annihilation of the enemy, no prisoners taken, the wounded shot and left for vultures to pick at.

"Ah well, it's a living.

"So...was CBS at all apprehensive about the expansion of *Dateline NBC* to 7 p.m. Sunday's opposite *60 Minutes*? Afraid of that pipsqueak, that ungrateful

The Clones

pretender of a newsmagazine that would not even be in existence were it not for the astonishing record of *60 Minutes* in pioneering this format? Nahhhhh."

Rosenberg chronicled several moves by CBS that indicated it had, indeed, been concerned, then reported the outcome.

"...Sunday's ratings found *60 Minutes* winning the hour with its usual-size audience. But *Dateline NBC* did dramatically inflate NBC's audience in that time period, running a respectable second by drawing viewers not from *60 Minutes*, it appeared, but from ABC (reruns of *America's Funniest Home Videos*) and Fox (reruns of *The Simpsons*)".

The actual numbers showed *60 Minutes* with a 15.6 rating to 9.4 for the Sunday *Dateline*. At that time, each rating point represented 959,000 homes. *60 Minutes* was the 8th ranked program that week, Sunday *Dateline* number 45. *Dateline* Tuesday, Friday and Wednesday, in that order, all finished higher than the new Sunday edition. What probably concerned both CBS and NBC was that *20/20* outpointed them both, ranking number four for the week with a 17.2 rating.

By mid-1996, *60 Minutes*, *20/20*, *Prime Time Live*, and *Dateline* were often all in the top 20, with two or even three of the *Dateline NBC* nights making the list. For the week of July 1-7, 1996, the highest rated program was an NBC movie, "Heart and Souls," with a 10.8 share of audience. After that, the Nielsen ratings looked like this:

2. *Prime Time Live*, ABC, 10.5
3. *20/20*, ABC, 10.4
4. *Dateline* (Tuesday), NBC, 10.4

Chapter Ten

    5. *Dateline* (Wednesday), NBC, 10.2
    6. *60 Minutes*, CBS, 9.9
    9. *Dateline* (Friday), NBC, 8.9

    Some consolation for *60 Minutes*, its direct competition, *Dateline* Sunday finished 39th, with a 6.5 share.

    Clearly the news magazines have become the mainstay of network programming. Just as clearly, *60 Minutes*, while still competitive, no longer dominates the field.

But what about...?

    There are legitimate news magazines that haven't been discussed here, some because they have come and gone, and some because they just aren't competitive. The tabloids, such as *Hard Copy* and *Inside Edition*, aren't included because they are "tabloids," little more related to a *60 Minutes* in content and presentation than the *National Enquirer* is related to *Time*. Because they are syndicated, rather than being carried by a network, they're not included in the same Nielsen ratings as the others, so audience comparisons are difficult. Finally, this book was intended to deal mainly with the problems of businesses faced with the "crisis" of being interviewed by a *60 Minutes*. Fairchild/Oppel so far has never recommended that a client agree to an interview with one of the tabloids. It is worthy of note, though, that some of these programs have moved away from their most sensational roots and have gained respectability in content and personnel. They may need to be looked at differently in the future. In 1997, *Inside Edition* won two prestigious journalism awards for an investigation into an insurance scam. But, even as the network news magazines dominated the ratings, the tabloids seemed to be losing ground. Associated Press reported that, at the same time it was winning those awards, *Inside Edition's* ratings had slipped 16 percent from the year before, "with *Hard Copy, Extra,* and *American Journal* also pulling fewer viewers. Only *Entertainment Tonight* has held its own."

What about *Nightline* or *Larry King*? What about the Sunday public affairs programs like Brinkley or *Meet the Press*? Their roots are different, *Meet the Press* even older than *60 Minutes*. They usually involve one subject at a time, instead of segments, and their interviews are usually live. Sometimes they use more than one guest at the same time.

We have prepared people for all of them, especially *Nightline* and *King*. Those differences offer some special problems, but the preparation techniques are basically the same. In spite of the dangers of being live, business spokespersons seem far less afraid of *Nightline* or *King* than of the edited magazine programs. Their biggest fear is still what that editor may take "out of context."

Chapter Eleven

Friend of Bill

The issues involved in our first *60 Minutes* program in 1982 were tough. Does Coors discriminate against just about everybody? Are the rights of employees routinely violated? Our job hasn't gotten any easier. Fifteen years later we had to prepare for an interview in which the question essentially was, "are you still bribing the President of the United States or did you stop that when he quit being governor of Arkansas?"

We became involved with Tyson Foods because of a *60 Minutes* program about another company. A program on conditions in the chicken processing industry focused on another Arkansas chicken processor, but generally indicted the whole industry for unsafe and unsanitary conditions. The threat of getting salmonella poisoning from eating chicken was emphasized as Diane

Chapter Eleven

Sawyer described a plant floor as "covered with fecal soup." Tyson Foods, headquartered in Springdale Arkansas, just a few miles from the plant that was the *60 Minutes* subject, is the undisputed leader in the chicken industry. Tyson executives knew this was the beginning, not the end, of the media assault, and they knew where to turn for help. Among Tyson's customers was a company well schooled in handling such problems. Tyson was the maker of that little chunk of white meat known as the "Chicken McNugget." They asked McDonald's to help them with a media relations program.

Robert L. Keyser was head of media relations for McDonald's at the time. In a similar job at Coors Beer, he had been the person who originally hired us to train Coors executives. He left Coors for McDonald's before the now-famous Coors *60 Minutes* program, but had been involved with the program several times since. Bob Keyser called in Fairchild/LeMaster and we set up a full scale training program for Tyson Foods in 1987.

As the company grew, Tyson faced a number of high profile issues, and, working with Keyser, we helped them deal with those issues in the media, but none actually involved *60 Minutes* until 1995. By then, the subject was potentially more dangerous than salmonella.

Keyser left McDonald's and started his own public relations consulting firm back in the state he and his family loved, Colorado. We continued to do media training for several of Bob's clients, including Tyson. The attention of the media, and the subject matter, reached new, undreamed of dimensions in 1992, with the election of Bill Clinton of Arkansas as President of the United States. Obviously the Clinton candidacy brought new media attention to Arkansas, and that meant attention to Tyson Foods as one of the state's largest employers. Keyser stepped up the company's media training program as the national media descended on the state. Safety standards, employee pay and benefits, waste products, community relations, virtually every possible aspect of the chicken business came under scrutiny and Tyson executives from plant managers on up were called upon to discuss those issues. Were chicken feathers polluting the Arkansas River? Was it humane to grow chickens from eggs to eating size without them ever leaving one of the long, low chicken houses that cover the landscape of northwest Arkansas like tobacco sheds cover North Carolina? Was the chicken manure that made northwest Arkansas lush green the year around leeching nitrogen into ground water? All those questions and more were addressed by the media during the 1992 election campaigns. Once Clinton became president, their attention turned to his relationship with Arkansas business. That had to include Tyson Foods, specifically its colorful CEO, Don Tyson.

Then in his sixties, Don Tyson was the son of the company's founder. He ran the multi-billion dollar company like a family business. His son and daughter were among the executives, but Don Tyson talked about all employees, a word he never used, as family. He proudly told stories about long-time Tyson "people" who became rich on the stock they routinely accumulated on a payroll stock plan. And, like his other top executives and rank and file workers, Don Tyson came to work

Chapter Eleven

every day in a khaki uniform with "Tyson" embroidered in red over the breast pocket.

I didn't know that when I went to Fayetteville to discuss our first training program. I knew I was to meet with the company president at their headquarters in nearby Springdale. I was pleased to see he had sent someone to meet me, a middle aged man in khaki uniform who walked me to his jeep.

"Welcome to Arkansas, Ken, I'm Leland Tollett," said the president of the company and the man who would succeed Don Tyson as chief executive when he retired.

The political questions increased geometrically from the time of Clinton's nomination. Tyson hired Archie Schaffer, a former congressional aide knowledgeable in politics and media. I thought Tyson, the company, was surprisingly neutral during the Clinton-Bush campaign. Anyone you asked would guess that Don Tyson was a big Clinton supporter, but there was no apparent pressure within the company to build support for the campaign. When Clinton won, there was no rush of Tyson executives to join the new administration in Washington. The fact was, Don Tyson had supported Clinton's first victorious campaign for governor of Arkansas, had become disenchanted and supported a Republican who unseated him, then backed Clinton's bid to reclaim the position. Considering that one was the state's top politician and the other was one of the two biggest businessmen in the state (Sam Walton, founder of Walmart, the other) Clinton and Tyson were far from close. But that was close enough for the media, and for some of Clinton's opponents in Congress. From Genifer Flowers to Whitewater, Clinton's relationships were subjected to microscopic scrutiny. Arkansas was awash with investigative reporters and Don Tyson

Friend of Bill

couldn't have avoided being one of their targets. One story, a true one, involved Hilary Clinton's dabbling in the commodities market. On the advice of the chief counsel of Tyson Foods, she had invested a relatively small amount and quickly reaped huge profits. The new secretary of agriculture, according to some stories handpicked for Clinton by Don Tyson, flew with his girl friend to a Dallas Cowboys football game on a Tyson plane, with Tyson tickets to the game. With absolutely no substantiation, there were stories of drugs being flown on Tyson planes and carried on Tyson trucks. All those stories and more were making the rounds at the time *60 Minutes* decided to do their Tyson story.

Bob Keyser didn't sound at all alarmed when he called to ask us to help prepare for the interview.

"I have a good relationship with the producer," he said. "We've had several conversations and a couple of meetings. They just want to do a profile on Don. You know, the good old boy from Arkansas."

As experienced as Keyser was in dealing with media, including *60 Minutes*, I felt a chill on the back of my neck. I had a hard time envisioning *60 Minutes* doing a friendly profile of Don Tyson and overlooking all those other things. "Let me see what the old computer says about the producer," I said. "Who is it?"

"Robert Anderson."

There he was at the top of the list. Anderson, Robert G. *. The asterisk meant watch out for dirty tricks.

"Our records say be careful, Bob. Let me see what caused us to put that in here."

The asterisk referred to the oldest information we had on Anderson. In September, 1990, he had produced "This House is a Steal," with Ed Bradley. It was the

127

Chapter Eleven

story of General Development Corporation in Florida, involving a disguised reporter and a parking lot ambush.

"Be careful, Bob."

Lisa LeMaster was even more concerned that the possible negatives were being taken too lightly. She urged Keyser and me to approach the interview with caution. She was especially concerned to learn that *60 Minutes* had invited Mike Wallace to accompany Don Tyson on a billfishing trip in the Caribbean. That was Tyson's biggest passion. At the time, one of the controversies involving Tyson and the Agriculture Department involved regulation of the chicken industry in Puerto Rico. Too easy to make a connection, we agreed. The fishing trip was replaced with a backyard cookout at Tyson's home in Arkansas. Keyser and I agreed we would approach our rehearsals for the interview the way we usually did, in expectation of the worst.

After the interview, Wallace would thank Keyser and Schaffer for not "over-preparing" Tyson. In fact, we did mock interviews on three separate occasions, twice in Springdale and once in Colorado at a Tyson company meeting. Playing the role of Mike Wallace, I pulled no punches. I asked about the rumors of drug smuggling, favors to the agriculture secretary and Tyson's personal relationship with President Clinton. Tyson's direct, honest answers were usually excellent, but not always.

"When he was governor, you and President Clinton must have attended a lot of functions together. Did you meet any of these women who have been mentioned in connection with him? Genifer flowers? Paula Jones?"

Tyson's eyes twinkled mischievously.

"No, I must have missed that one."

We all agreed that might not be the best answer if Wallace asked a similar question.

We knew who CBS was talking to around Arkansas, and what questions they were asking. We were pretty sure that this information, plus common sense and an understanding of the media, made it possible for us to anticipate the questions Wallace would ask. Our main goal was to show that Don Tyson's relationship with Bill Clinton was not unusual, certainly not close enough for Tyson to wield the kind of influence that was being implied. Keyser, Schaffer and I agreed that our objectives boiled down to a couple of key points. We wanted Tyson to come across as himself, and we wanted to show that he had been as close to other presidents, and was as close to other governors, as he had been to Bill Clinton. The basic message was that all of the allegations, all of the attention, were really aimed at embarrassing President Clinton, not at Don Tyson.

The program opened with Mike Wallace in front of a picture of a smiling Tyson over large letters, F. O. B.?

"Don't call Don Tyson an F. O. B. Most people would love to be known as a friend of Bill's. Knowing the president is heady stuff. But Don Tyson says it's been mostly headaches for him. You see, Don Tyson is a billionaire chicken plucker from Arkansas. He runs the world's biggest chicken company, Tyson Foods, a five billion dollar business. The national press keeps reporting that Tyson is a very good F. O. B, and that Tyson keeps asking the President for favors for his company. Tyson insists that's simply not true. But he says that trying to get a reporter to correct a mistake is like kicking a skunk. Usually, you just smell worse. He complains that reports about favors and influence are

Chapter Eleven

hurting his company's image, and finally he got so steamed about it he invited us down to his world headquarters in Springdale, Arkansas, to set the record straight."

Then comes the first clip, the first sound bite. It's Don Tyson, smiling, but intense.

"I've seen the President twice in two years—twice in two years—once in Arkansas on a social occasion and once on Saturday morning when I was doing the White House tour and didn't even have an appointment. You know, I was just walking through the White House on Saturday morning."

Watching at home, heart in throat as it always is on these occasions, I hissed, "yessss." You wouldn't have to have been involved in nineteen *60 Minutes* programs to know this was not the start of a hatchet job. At the very least, our side of the story would be told.

Wallace told the story of Tyson's backing of Clinton in his first election as governor, only to take the other side in the next election because he thought Clinton had not kept a promise to support trucking legislation that would have been good for Tyson. Clinton lost. The next time around, Tyson switched back, Clinton was elected to another term—and the trucking legislation was passed.

"You seem to go to great pains," said Wallace, "to minimize your clout with Bill Clinton. Why?"

"'Cause I don't have any," Tyson laughed.

"None?"

"None. I think he might answer my phone call in two or three days."

"But you've never called him."

"I've never called him, so I don't have to test him."

"A lot of people would say, yeah, I know Bill Clinton."

"I do know him. I know the governor of Texas. I know the governor of Oklahoma. I know the governor of Tennessee. That's part of my job."

From that exchange, which scored our major objective for the program, Wallace went to a description of the company, it's dominance in the industry and the story of how Don's father started the business. Then Wallace moved back to the question of influence, Tyson frankly admitting that he spends money to support politicians who will be favorable to Tyson and the industry.

Wallace: "You spend money to make money. So, if you spend money on politicians, obviously you hope you're going to make money because you have spent money on politicians, right?"

Tyson: "Not to make money. Just to make sure you get a fair shake if you have a problem."

Wallace: "And the more money you give, chances are you're going to get a better shake because they're going to listen more carefully to somebody who's a big contributor..."

Tyson: "I hope so."

Wallace: "Anything wrong with that?"

Tyson: "I don't see it. It's part of our system, and I believe it's part of my responsibility."

So far, so good. Though the point of political contributions in return for influence had clearly been made, Tyson's candor, at least in my opinion, had

Chapter Eleven

neutralized the issue so far. Now, though, Wallace turned to the subject of Michael Espy, the embattled Secretary of Agriculture. Tyson had to admit that he should have asked Espy to pay for his Cowboys tickets up front, instead of after the fact and after the issue became public. There was no answer to the fact that Tyson had never been reimbursed for the expenses of Espy's girl friend. Tyson admitted having had lunch with Espy before his appointment by the President, after which, Wallace said, Tyson sent word to Washington that Espy would be fine for Secretary of Agriculture.

Wallace: "How much influence do you have over secretary of agriculture Espy?"
Tyson: "None."
Wallace: "None?"
Tyson: "None."

Wallace joined Tyson in the company cafeteria, pointing out that Tyson's emphasis on profitability led him to install an electronic stock ticker in that room.

Wallace: "If I'd invested a thousand dollars in Tyson Foods , say twenty-five years ago, what would it be worth today?"
Tyson: "A half million dollars."
Wallace: "Five hundred times?"
Tyson: "Yeah."
Wallace: "In twenty-five years?"
Tyson: "Yeah. Isn't that great?"
Wallace: "If you'd persuaded Mrs. Clinton instead of buying commodity futures, to buy Tyson stock..."
Tyson: "She'd a been a lot better off."
Wallace: "Yeah."

Friend of Bill

Tyson: "But I didn't know her then."

That was Wallace' way of introducing the subject of Hillary Clinton's much discussed killing in the commodities market on the advice of Jim Blair, described by Wallace as the Clinton's closest friend and Tyson's company attorney. Tyson had already made one of two points we considered to be important in handling that issue, that he hadn't known Mrs. Clinton then. Our second major point had already been made—by Mike Wallace. Mrs. Clinton would have been better off buying Tyson stock.

That set up what to me was the climax of the segment, the coup de grace.

Wallace: " 'Course the story went around that this was a payoff from Tyson to the governor's wife. You've heard this."
Tyson: "Oh, yeah. Not true."
Wallace: "In no way true."
Tyson: "No," and a second time, "I didn't know Mrs. Clinton then."
Wallace: "Then why do you think this story keeps going around?"
Tyson: "If we lived in Oklahoma, you wouldn't be here."
Wallace: "That's true, and it's what, forty miles away?"
Tyson: "Yes sir."
Wallace: "That's true."
Tyson: "And the other thing is, I think a lot of this is just to embarrass the President."

133

Chapter Eleven

Wallace then made another of our points.

"Tyson was actually closer to President Carter than he was to President Clinton. After Tyson visited Carter in the oval office years ago, he redesigned his office to look like the President's, but instead of oval, he calls it 'egg shaped.'"

But there are always reminders that one can never make the mistake of assuming that Wallace, or anyone else at *60 Minutes*, has mellowed, or been won over. The other side, the critical side, will always get it's best shots as well.

Wallace: "We've spoken to people, and I'm sure you know this, who have called you, and I quote: ruthless, amoral, unscrupulous, mean spirited, but they wouldn't come on camera and say that because they're afraid of you and your power."

Tyson: "Well, the best thing for 'em to do is call me up and I'll give 'em my phone number and let's go talk about it."

Wallace cites Tyson's characterization of himself as "the toughest son of a gun in the valley, except that you used another word. What makes you so tough?"

"In business, it seems like nice guys run last."

And the final exchange of the program is yet another characterization of Don Tyson.

Wallace: "You said, Don, that the one word that sums you up is 'fun.'"
Tyson: "Yes sir."
Wallace: "What's fun?"
Tyson: "Fun's coming to work in the morning.

Friend of Bill

Fun's making things happen. Funs giving opportunity to people. I think the greatest thing about America is we can all do what my dad did—start a business."

My phone rang a few minutes after the program. It was Don Tyson. He was very pleased with the outcome, thanked me for my help, and bestowed what may be the supreme accolade of my career.

"You were much tougher than Mike Wallace," he said.

I have a reminder of that conversation on my desk—a gift from Tyson. It's a nearly-life-size Lalique crystal rooster that looks like he's probably the toughest son of a gun in the valley.

An article in *Arkansas Business* following the broadcast left no doubt that the writer considered it a Tyson victory. It quoted Archie Schaffer as saying, "I think the main reason it went well is because Don Tyson is what he is and appears to be on *60 Minutes*—an honest, straightforward businessman."

Chapter Eleven

Messages from Arkansas

No matter what they tell you, err on the side of being too careful. Learn what can be learned from producers and interviewers. Assume they're truthful and want to be helpful. Plan accordingly. Then prepare for the worst. Take no chances. As my old pappy used to say, *"trust everyone, but always cut the cards."*

Know when to prepare and when to quit. The right amount of preparation is whatever it takes to make the spokesperson able to deliver key messages while fighting off the toughest questions, all the while appearing comfortable and at ease. Over-preparing can cause the exact opposite, a spokesperson who seems wooden, spouting messages that appear memorized.

Forget gilded lilies and silk purses. Even the "Great Communicator," Ronald Reagan could be pushed too far. When that happened, his closest friends and advisors screamed, "let Reagan be Reagan!" The goal must be to make the spokesperson come across as naturally as possible.

Chapter twelve

Should I, or Shouldn't I?

Despite a drastic decline in total audience, in spite of strong competition, *60 Minutes* continues to enjoy a mystique the others don't have. When we get a call from someone saying they need help because they're going to be interviewed by *60 Minutes*, there is a quiver in the voice we don't hear when the program is *Dateline*, or *20/20*. We obviously share some of that awe. We know exactly how many *60 Minutes* programs we've been involved in. We haven't kept track of the *Nightlines*, or *Prime Time Live*s. *Dateline*, with it's three and sometimes four nights a week to fill, has become a mini-industry for us in itself. In one recent three-week period, we were involved in preparation for seven separate *Dateline* segments. But when I tell seminars we have worked on more than twenty *60 Minutes* programs, there is inevitably a gasp.

Chapter Twelve

For one thing, the perception American business has of the news media has changed hardly at all during the lifetime of *60 Minutes*. Think of how the media have changed in the last thirty years. There were no satellites making it possible to cover events around the world live, and for local stations to send their own reporters to cover those events anywhere. There was no CNN. Watergate had not yet spawned a generation of "investigative" reporters. The prevailing attitude of business people, outside the communications departments, seemed to be, "The less we talk to them the better. They'll just take anything we say and turn it against us." Communications executives often described their jobs as to "protect" or "defend" the company image. That was the attitude toward all media. No wonder the proverbial call from Mike Wallace provoked terror.

Thirty years later, there is no more trust between business and media than there was then. In February, 1996, Peter Johnson, writer of an "Inside TV" column for *USA Today,* reported on a survey of 300 executives by "Elective Voice on Media", which, he said, "examines how exec's deal with information sources."

"The survey, focusing on 26 print and electronic outlets, found exec's most skeptical about newsmags and newscasts.

"They prefer trade journals, business magazines and programs such as PBS' *Jim Lehrer News Hour* (fourth on the list), ABC's *This Week with David Brinkley* (6) and NBC's *Meet the Press* (10).

"Bottom six: *Dateline* (21), *60 Minutes* (22), *NBC Nightly News*, (23), *20/20* (24), *CBS Evening News* (25) and ABC's *Prime Time Live* (26).

"Exec's surveyed believe newsmags and newscasts 'don't go into enough depth. And when they do focus on

Should I, or Shouldn't I?

business, it's usually negative,' says Alan Siegel, who designed the survey."

I've heard those exact words from business people for twenty years as a media consultant, and I heard them for fifteen years before that as a reporter and news director. My point is not that the media are any more deserving of trust today, but that business people should have learned some things in these thirty years that would make the media less alien, less intimidating. They haven't. One ironic point in that survey. *Prime Time Live* is the least trusted of all. Why? Your guess, as mine, would probably be two words—Sam Donaldson. Facing his pit bull style is probably not high on the list of what any executive would do for fun. But notice, *This Week with David Brinkley* is, at number six on the list, one of the most respected programs. Of course Sam Donaldson plays a major role on that program! What's the difference? In his *USA Today* column, Johnson asked Donaldson that question.

"Let's face it," he answered, "they don't like to see expose´s we do that are aimed at business practices. They feel we're either unfair or wrong." As for the Brinkley program, "we have a lot of discussion about government policies that affect business. I would imagine questions we put to Pat Buchanan about (him being) anti-business, anti-free trade—(exec's) would think that was responsible reporting. Talk to Buchanan's folks, and they'll say the devils are at work."

Donaldson's analysis is probably correct. We all tend to view the media as "right" or "wrong" depending on whose side the devils are on. As we learned in our first *60 Minutes* exposure, when Mike Wallace pointed his finger at the union official leading the Coors boycott and

Chapter Twelve

said, "that's really the crux of the matter, isn't it? They threw out the union," it's great when the devils are on your side. Because business people view the media that way, though, it is easy to want to play it safe, to avoid any media contact that isn't initiated by our own PR department. Even then, many executives prefer not to do interviews. "Let the press release speak for itself. They might ask tough questions about other things."

Should we, or shouldn't we? When *60 Minutes* or *Dateline* calls, should we even consider cooperating? Here are two simple questions to ask ourselves that will help make that decision:

Is it really our story? If it's an industry story, not specifically related to our company, we have every right to decline the honor of participating. That decision should be made based on the answers to further questions: will we gain stature by being identified as the industry spokespersons? Is there a possibility that bad news that doesn't apply to us might appear to refer to us if we are involved? Is there someone else we can refer them to that can fill their need and reflect well on us?

Do we have a story to tell? We should have a clear vision of our goal for the interview. If we're really bad guys, maybe we shouldn't give the media a chance to prove it. The decision must not be based on whether the potential story is good or bad, favorable or unfavorable, but on whether we have something to say that will make it better, that will present us in a more favorable light than if we are not represented.

If the answer to those questions is "yes," then we probably should take part. Arguments against doing so are often, "if we are involved, we'll only make it a bigger story," or the corollary, "if we don't take part, maybe it will go away (maybe they won't do the story)."

Should I, or Shouldn't I?

Right, and I'm from the IRS, I'm here to help you; the check is in the mail; and I'll respect you in the morning. If it is truly bad news, or if it's really news at all, it won't go away. I have never known of a situation in which a story was killed simply because one party, especially the potential target, refused to be interviewed.

In our opinion, the risks of refusing to talk to the media on a serious issue are greater than the risks of being interviewed; but just what are the risks, the actual risks to the bottom line, of being exposed to (or on) *60 Minutes*?

In 1985, three professors at North Texas State University (now the University of North Texas) researched the question of how much *60 Minutes* exposes (their word) "affect the wealth of stockholders of a company." P. R. Chandy and Wallace N. Davidson, III, were associate professors and Sharon Garrison assistant professor of business administration. They used respected research methods well documented in their report. They examined twenty nine *60 Minutes* broadcasts involving corporations. After eliminating those involving companies that were subsidiaries of others, those whose securities trade infrequently, and private companies that didn't trade at all, they were left with a sample of thirteen companies. Among those was our Coors broadcast and a program on the "Tylenol murders." Others involved the Dalkon Shield and Dow Chemical and complaints of health problems, deaths from a drug, waste and fraud in government contracts, and similar examples of typical *60 Minutes* fare (see appendix for complete list and more specific details of the research).

The researchers examined the activity of each

141

Chapter Twelve

company's stock the week before and week after the broadcast, volume of shares traded, closing prices and volatility. They also calculated what they called abnormal returns and cumulated abnormal returns for a period of ten weeks before, to 15 weeks after, the broadcast. Their conclusion:

"There did appear to be a market reaction to the news. The surprise is that the impact is not negative; on the contrary, it is positive. The AR. (abnormal return) on week 1, the week of the broadcast, is especially striking, with a very large AR."

In other words, the stocks went up.

"Our examination of the data on a daily basis provided similar results. ...the greatest impact occurred over the two days immediately following the broadcast, but the drift in a (cumulative abnormal return) is upward over the 15-day period following the broadcast.

"This confirms the earlier finding that, if anything, the market reacts *favorably* (emphasis in the original) to the 60 Minutes news, even though the information broadcast was negative for companies in the sample."

Was it? Though the conclusion that the market invariably went up seems to be a fact, the statement that all the information that was broadcast was negative, or the researchers' conclusions that the programs they examined were mostly negative toward the corporations, are open to question. While the original premise of the Coors program was negative, the program content was balanced. The researchers example of a "positive " program is interesting as well.

"After going through the transcripts of 60 Minutes," the research paper says, "we found the show presented only one firm— Johnson and Johnson—in a positive framework. All other firms had negative information

142

Should I, or Shouldn't I?

presented in the show..."

The subject of the Johnson and Johnson program is listed in the research paper as "an inside view of Johnson and Johnson's efforts to market Tylenol after the 'Tylenol murders.'"

A discussion of murders committed with a company's product and its viewed as "positive!"

"This study shows that the market did not react negatively to events we studied for which the informational content could be regarded as negative. The sample size is admittedly small, so a possible explanation is that one or two companies might have influenced the results. But when the security prices were examined around the broadcast date for each of the companies, the pattern of abnormal returns was found to be general...we can reject the notion that one or two companies overly influenced the results.

"A second possible explanation addresses the broadcasts themselves. Perhaps the broadcasts were not negative, but instead were about positive features of the companies. To this end, we examined the transcripts of the programs from CBS. While our analysis of the transcripts was objective, each of the three authors independently found the tone of all the broadcasts except one to be negative.

"The one exception was the Johnson and Johnson broadcast.... While Johnson and Johnson was not treated negatively, the story showed the tremendous liability that the company was facing as well as its commendable efforts to improve the safety of the product. In any event, Johnson and Johnson's returns did not overly influence the results. We could not see

Chapter Twelve

any difference between these returns and those of the stocks for which there were more negative stories."

Even if murder is not negative enough, there are those businessmen and women who would consider a story that "showed the tremendous liability the company was facing" to be very negative. My point is not to argue with the learned researchers, but to point out that where their conclusions are subjective, their judgment is skewed exactly as Sam Donaldson described. It all depends on whether the media appears to be doing the devil's work. No one accused Tylenol of being culpable in the "Tylenol murders." They were, in fact, treated as a sympathetic figure, a victim themselves. On the other hand, the researchers cite Coors as an example of a negative story while all of us associated with the Coors side considered it a tremendous victory and *60 Minutes* treatment as fair and even handed. But the subject was, as the researchers described, "stories that the company is 'anti-black, anti-women, anti-homosexual and that's just for starters.' From a business standpoint, such a program, however balanced, must seem like the devil's work.

The North Texas researchers added a third possible explanation for their surprising results.
"The positive results suggest the broadcasts cleared the air about whatever problems the companies were having. In other words, even though the stories were negative, they were already known. The broadcasts may have provided news that was less negative than previous news stories. In addition, CBS and *60 Minutes* allow companies to present their side of the story. This

Should I, or Shouldn't I?

may, in fact, be the first and/or the best chance that the company will have to defend itself to the public at large.

"The market may react favorably to the broadcast because *60 Minutes* reduces uncertainty about the company's problems and other related issues...

"All in all, if you are met at the door by the *60 Minutes* crew, the day may not be as bad as you once thought—at least not for your investors."

Does it make a difference if it's *20/20* calling, or *Dateline*?

In our opinion the thought process in deciding to take part should be the same, whether it's *60 Minutes*, the *New York Times*, or the local news. Are some more dangerous than others? Sure. As we've already mentioned, the pressures of producing four *Dateline* programs a week may mean less time for research. The very proliferation of magazine programs may mean lower standards of reporting and producing, just as baseball expansion meant more .250 hitters on major league rosters. That simply means we have to be more careful in answering those questions to decide— should we, or shouldn't we.

Chapter thirteen

A Strategy for Winning

We have decided we have a story to tell. We have agreed to an interview. Now what?
Whether it's *60 Minutes* or the local news, the answers should be the same. While the name and reputation of *60 Minutes* and others of its genre strike fear in most hearts, interviews with local newspapers and TV are equally, and often more, dangerous. Local reporters, producers and editors may be less experienced than their network counterparts. They will almost certainly have less time to develop a story or to learn the background information surrounding it. Yet within their coverage area, they have all the power, the impact, of CBS or the *New York Times*. Every interview should be approached as if it's *60 Minutes* on the line. That's not meant to imply that all interviews are going to be negative or even potentially dangerous, but any

Chapter Thirteen

interview worth doing should be worth preparing for. The outcome does not have to be left in the hands of the gods, or of the editors.

The message   In the 1970s, Marshall McLuhan wrote a book called *The Medium is the Message.* He said, essentially, that television is a medium of such impact that how a person comes across on the tube is more important than what the person has to say. In the late '80s, Roger Ailes wrote a book called *You Are the Message,* that placed somewhat more importance on the words, but still emphasized the effects of personality on the audience.

We think the *message* is the message. A poor presentation can certainly detract from, maybe destroy, the credibility of a message, but no performance, no matter how slick, can get a message across if the words aren't there. In fact, the emphasis on personality of McLuhan, Ailes and others, has led to a proliferation of performances, especially by politicians, that leave the audience doubting the credibility of the speaker. Most audiences today won't buy style without substance. Style helps sell, all right, but it pays to start with substance—the message.

Why are we doing this interview? What do we want to say? What do we want the soundbite to be? Decide on the message as if it will be limited to a single sentence, one headline. Now what would we add if we could have a full paragraph or a full minute on television?

The biggest fear we have of media is the fear that "they," reporters or editors, will use only a small part of what we say. That will happen. Then the complaint is often, "they chose the wrong part, the wrong ten seconds, out of what I said." Put more simply, we say,

A Strategy for Winning

"they quoted me out of context." That means, "of course I said it, but it wasn't the part I thought they would use." Yet virtually every person we have worked with over the years has said, "but my story, our story, our business, is too complex to explain in ten seconds (or two minutes, or ten minutes)."

Think about it. If our biggest fear is that "they" will choose the wrong part of what we say, why would the answer be, "if only I could give them more choices?"

Our goal in developing our message must be to limit those choices. That means we must be direct, succinct, clear in our meaning, and—quotable. No amount of time or number of words will get our story told in the media if we don't tell it in a quotable way.

Answers

Only after we've decided on the message and couched it in the most quotable terms, should we begin to consider what questions the reporter will ask. We must answer those questions. To avoid them, to say no comment, to be too glib or clever, will destroy our credibility. *But don't over-answer.* We tend to spend more time answering the toughest questions, the ones we'd rather not be answering at all. In preparing a witness for trial testimony, we stress that most court cases are not *won* during cross examination, but they *can* be *lost* there.

Consider the shortest, best, honest answer to each anticipated question. Recognize that the question doesn't have to be answered to the satisfaction of the reporter. The goal is not to educate or convince the interviewer, but to answer the question and move on to the message whenever possible.

Chapter Thirteen

Bridging

Developers of the original spokesperson training program in the early '70s called the process of answering a question and moving to the message, "bridging." The technique worked so well that most of those who have copied it over the years have treated it (and in some cases, taught it) as a miraculous way to avoid answering questions. The result can be seen on television news almost every night as someone launches into a canned answer, seemingly unrelated to the question. It doesn't work that way. Audiences hardened by years of seeing politicians answer a question that wasn't asked are used to dismissing that technique.

Bridging was always supposed to mean answer the question, then move to the applicable message. Those early-'70s ancestors of the modern "spin doctor" had no idea that their concept would work so well that it would be co-opted by the dark side. The goal was to give business people the courage to go on television and *answer* questions, not to raise false hopes that questions could be ignored altogether and audiences would be too stupid or naive to notice.

Some of our would-be competitors teach "ignore the question and say what you came to say." Some talk about how to avoid questions, block questions, get away from questions. Some provide ready-made "transitions," all purpose bridging phrases like "the real issue here is..." or "that's a good question, but..." some go on from there to suggest asking yourself a question you like better. "What you should be asking is...", or "a better question might be...". That last one is a sure fire way *not* to win friends in the media.

Answer the darn question! If you don't know the answer, say so. If you can't answer for some other

A Strategy for Winning

reason, explain why not. Then, and only then, bridge to the positive message. That's how simple the bridging concept really is: *listen* to the question, give the *short, honest* answer, go to what you're *prepared* to say on that subject. The technique is simple, but success or failure really depends on that word "prepared." We're often approached by people facing a critical situation, a *60 Minutes* interview or a political debate, who ask, "can you teach me how to think on my feet in a situation like that?"

The answer is no.

You should never have to make up answers on your feet, which really means off the top of your head. Political debates, political campaigns, media battles, are not won by the person who is most glib, but by the person who is best prepared and keeps the battle on his or her turf. That means pick your battle, then stick to the game plan.

Who and where?

We may disagree with McLuhan and Ailes over whether the *medium* is the message, *you* are the message, or the *message* is the message, but it is unarguable that the person doing the interview and the location of the interview play an important role in determining credibility of the message. That's especially true in dealing with television. How often have we seen the widow or child, environmental activist or disgruntled ex-employee, emotionally telling a story, then to be rebutted by the classic, gray-haired, white male executive? It's those situations that led McLuhan and Ailes to their conclusions about the importance of presentation over message. While I believe strongly that

Chapter Thirteen

nothing matters if the message isn't there, it certainly doesn't help to dig such a hole to start with, to begin with such a disadvantage when it comes to getting that message through to the audience. The spokesperson's position or title becomes part of the message. The choice of a public relations person to answer media questions can send the wrong signals as to the importance and even the veracity of the answers. Using an attorney or corporate counsel to respond sends a message of its own, and quite often ends up with short comments in legalese that either sound guilty or don't get quoted anyway because they are deliberately unresponsive.

The spokesperson should be someone with a title or position that conveys expertise on the matter at hand. That person then must be prepared well enough to be confident and to show that confidence in the interview. It doesn't always have to be the CEO. How high up the ladder the spokesperson should be is a strategic decision. It may be that the CEO is the right choice, if the issue is important enough that it must be dealt with at the highest level, and, if doing so will help lay the matter to rest. It may be, though, that the opposite is true. The issue may be one that would best be confined to a local response at a lower level. That leaves open the possibility of moving to a higher level if necessary, what Admiral Poindexter, during the Iran-Contra hearings, called, "plausible deniability." It's usually possible to move a response to a higher level for clarification or further information, but it's difficult to make it work the other way, to have a subordinate trying to explain what the CEO really meant. Women, especially women with high-level executive positions, are being used more and more in such spokesperson roles, and with good results. Women usually convey a warmth or empathy that is

A Strategy for Winning

missing in their male counterparts.

Finally, the location of the interview is part of the message. Our basic rule in crisis communication is, if it's good news, get the company logo in the background. If it's bad news, don't. If the plant is on fire, we don't have to stand in front of the fire to tell our story. We don't have to do an interview in front of a line of chanting protesters or pickets, even though it makes great television. Again, it's a strategic decision. An interview in a quiet office might be the best response, but having an executive talking to the pickets, perhaps taking them coffee, might convey our message better. The interview should take place in a location that helps tell our story, where the spokesperson will be comfortable and in control, and where he or she will have access to any information that might be needed during the interview. Those points are just as important in a print interview as they are for television.

Executing the game plan

Tom Landry, at the height of his success as coach of the Dallas Cowboys, often commented that he had noticed that the team that worked the hardest during the week always seemed to be the luckiest on Sunday. No matter how good the talent, no matter how good the game plan, they won't win the game without practice and execution. The same is true in doing a media interview. Preparation for an important interview, television or print, should include simulated, "practice" interviews, anticipating as nearly as possible the toughest questions likely to be asked. Then, at game time, the key is execution. All the preparation in the

Chapter Thirteen

world, even with adequate practice, goes down the drain without execution, and execution depends on discipline. Once the interview starts, all the thinking and planning and positioning is in the hands of the spokesperson. Success depends on that person's determination to stick to the planned, positive messages and to avoid fighting the wrong battles.

When it all comes together—the hard work, the planning, trying to outguess the other guy, the practice, fighting back the fear—and the defense is beaten for the winning touchdown, there must be nothing like the feeling of the one who scores, and wins. Ask Joe and Bill Coors, or Ed Hess, or Don Tyson. As for those of us who make a career regularly skirting the edge of media disaster, there's never time to savor victory. There's another program next week—three segments, plus Andy Rooney—, and between now and then, *Prime Time Live, 20/20,* a fistful of *Datelines, Nightline,* and who knows, maybe a *Hard Copy* or *Inside Edition, Today Show* or *Good Morning America,* even an *Oprah,* and don't forget the *Wall Street Journal,* and *New York Times.*

God, I love this job!

Appendix

60 Minutes program segments included in the study by P. R. Chandy, Wallace N. Davidson, III, and Sharon Garrison of North Texas State University at Denton, Texas. The study, published in 1985, was entitled "Bad news = good news! Who can tell?" Comments/program descriptions are theirs.

Firestone, 03/08/81, Killer Wheels. Story examines deaths attributed to allegedly dangerous wheel rims.

Goodyear 03/08/81, Killer Wheels. Story examines deaths attributed to allegedly dangerous wheel rims.

A. H. Robbins, 04/19/81, The Dalkon Shield. Purports that the Dalkon Shield IUD is linked to "at least 16 deaths and innumerable lawsuits."

SmithKline, 02/07/82, The Bad Drug. Company officials allegedly failed to report to the FDA problems with the drug Selaryn which may have been "the cause of about 60 deaths and over a thousand patients...."

Rockwell International, 03/07/82, The Money Shuttle. An examination of whether Rockwell illegally padded costs of the space shuttle contract.

General Electric, 03/07/82, Out of Work. G. E. closes a metal iron plant in Ontario and devastates workers, even though the plant was profitiable.

Martin Marietta, 09/05/82, Titan. Titan missiles are depicted as unnecessary as well as dangerous.

Adolph Coors, 09/26/82, Trouble Brewing. Boycotts against Coors Beer because of stories that the company is "anti-black, anti-women, anti-homosexual and that's just for starters" caused sales to drop sharply.

Johnson & Johnson, 12/19/82, The Re-Selling of Tylenol. An inside view of Johnson & Johnson's efforts to market Tylenol after the "Tylenol murders."

Amex Corp., 03/13/83, The Thomas Reed Affair. Thomas Reed, a former secretary of the Air Force is alleged to have illegally profited from inside trading violations in Amex Corporation.

Dow Chemical, 03/13/83, The Spraying of Moundville. Citizens of Moundville, Alabama complain of health problems after the town was sprayed with a herbicide made by Dow Chemical.

Eli Lilly, 04/17/83, Oraflex. Company officials "knew about more than two dozen deaths and failed to report them... ."

Litton Industries, 04/24/83, Dollars Aweigh. Outlines charges of waste and fraud at the Ingalls Shipbuilding Division of Litton Industries.

INDEX

ABC	21, 43, 63, 68, 70, 112, 113, 115-117, 119, 138
ABC Town Hall	96
AFL-CIO	5, 8, 12
Agriculture, Department of	128
Agriculture, Secretary of	127, 128, 132
Ailes, Roger	15, 148, 151
America's Funniest Home Videos	119
American Journal	121
Anderson, Robert G.	46, 74, 127
Arab oil embargo	19
Argentina	65
Arkansas	123, 125-130
Arkansas Business	135
Arkansas River	125
Associated Press	20, 121
Bark, Ed	116, 117
Bergman, Lowell	74
Black, Jonathan	63, 73
Blair, Jim	133
Blue Cross and Blue Shield	102, 104, 106-108
Blue Cross/Blue Shield Association	83-86, 88, 90, 91, 93, 95-101, 104, 105, 107, 108, 110
Boston, Massachusetts	21, 65
Bradley, Ed	xi, xii, 42, 46, 47, 55, 56, 62, 65, 66, 68, 69, 72, 74, 78, 79, 114, 127
Brady, James	69
"Brezhnev's Daughter"	80
Brinkley, David	121, 138, 139
Brokaw, Tom	114
Buchanan, Pat	139
"Bug Man"	42
Burella, Jerry	14
Bush, President George	15, 98, 126
Camera Shy	21
Carlson, Duane	83-88, 90-92, 97, 98, 100
Carlson, Richard	58
Carter, President Jimmy	134
Chandy, P. R.	141
Channels magazine	55, 63, 73, 75

157

Chicago 79
Chicago, Illinois 79, 85, 88, 90, 96, 97
Chicken McNugget 124
Chung, Connie 114, 116, 117
CIA 79
Clinton, First Lady Hillary Rodham 65, 69, 96, 99, 117, 127, 133
Clinton, Illinois 54
Clinton, President Bill 69, 95-97, 125-130, 132-134
Colorado 124, 128
Concord 102
confrontational journalism 23, 25
Congress, United States 43, 67, 95-97, 126
Conroe, Texas 57
Coors Company, Adolph 1-19, 21-23, 33, 37, 39, 50, 64, 74, 75,
                              92, 123, 124, 139, 141, 142, 144, 155
Coors, Bill 1, 2, 4, 6-8, 10-12, 15, 17, 25, 154
Coors, Jeff 2, 6
Coors, Joe 1, 2, 4, 6-8, 10, 15, 154
Coors, Pete 2, 6
Couric, Katie 117
"Critic, The" 80
Cronkite, Walter 22, 68
Cubans 44
Dalkon Shield 141
"Dallas" 31
Dallas Cowboys 127, 132, 153
Dallas Morning News 116
Dallas, Texas .... vii, 2, 11, 13, 55, 56, 85
Dateline NBC .... vii, 115-120, 137, 138, 140, 145, 154
Davidson, Wallace N., III 141
Day One 116, 117
deBoismilon, Anne 74
Defense Department 43
Denver, Colorado 3, 14
Diconcini, Dennis 25, 67
Dingell, Congressman John 43, 45
documentaries 111
"Doing Business with City Hall" 79
Donaldson, Sam 9, 21, 61, 70, 112, 113, 139, 144
Dow Chemical 141
Downey, Morton, Jr. 112, 113
Downs, Hugh 61, 112, 114
energy crisis 4
Entertainment Tonight 121
Environmental Protection Agency 33

Erlichman, John	85
Espy, Michael	132
Evening News	67, 68, 114
Ewing, J. R.	56
Expose´	114, 115
Extra	121
Exxon	29-32, 36, 37
Eye to Eye With Connie Chung	114, 116
Face the Nation	111
Fairchild, Ken	91, 126
Fairchild/LeMaster	2, 44, 69, 113, 124
Fairchild/Oppel	73, 120
Fayetteville, Arkansas	126
57th Street	59, 114, 115
Fine, Holly	55
Fine, Paul	55
Florida	46, 66, 79
Flowers, Genifer	126, 128
"F. O. B."	129
Food and Drug Administration	42
Ford, President Gerald	67
48 Hours	114-117
Four White Knights	63
Fox network	115-117, 119
Franklin, Aretha	65
Freedom Financial Corporation	55-57
Frey, Doug	44
Front Line	116
Front Page	117
Galloway, Dr. Carl	59
Garrison, Sharon	141
General Development Corporation of Florida	46, 47, 128
Gengrich, Congressman Newt	114
Georgia	96
Gerstner, Bill	51-53
Gettysburg Address	89
Giraldo	113
Glen, Alixe	98-100, 102, 104, 107, 108
Golden, Colorado	2, 3
Good Morning America	154
Governor of Arkansas	123, 126, 128
Governor of Oklahoma	131
Governor of Tennessee	131
Governor of Texas	131

Graham, Sandy	54
Grenada, Island of	44
Hannaford, Peter	15, 59
Hard Copy	77, 120, 121, 154
Hartman, Rome	78
Hassler, Patti	74, 78
healthcare	96-98
"Heart and Souls"	119
Henson, Jim	80
Hess, Ed	32, 33, 36, 154
Hewitt, Don	v, 23-25, 27, 59, 62-64, 67-70, 75, 111, 116, 117
Hilton, Jack	21, 22
Hong Kong	65, 99
Horne, Lena	65
Houston Chronicle	57
Houston, Texas	29, 31
Howard, Josh	74
Hudson River	21
"If Push Comes to Shove"	80
Illinois Commerce Commission	52
Illinois Power Company	50, 51, 53, 54, 58, 60, 78, 91
Inside Edition	77, 120, 154
Inside TV	138
IRS	106, 107
Jarriel, Tom	112
Jeep	126
Jim Lehrer News Hour	138
Johnson and Johnson	142, 143
Johnson, Peter	138, 139
Jones, Paula	128
Keyser, Robert L.	124, 125, 127-129
KGB	79
Klaus, Marley	74, 78, 79
Kroft, Steve	42, 62, 68, 69, 72
Lando, Barry	74
Landry, Tom	153
Lang, Bob	84, 89-92
Larry King	121
Las Colinas, Texas	108
LeMaster, Lisa	2, 3, 5, 7, 9, 11, 29-31, 128
Lewis, Parker	117
Liddy, Gordon	85
Loewenwarter, Paul	51, 53
London, England	74

Los Angeles Times	118
Los Angeles, California	59, 66
LULAC	6, 12
LUST	30, 32, 38
Mafia	42
mail-order minister	63
managed care	96
Maraynes, Alan	11, 15, 23, 74, 75
marijuana	14
Marine Corps	44
MCA	42
McCarty, John	1
McDonald's poration	40, 41, 124
McGraw Hill	85
McLuhan, Marshall	148, 151
Mead, Bob	56, 57
Meadows, John	1-3, 5, 6, 9, 14, 17
meat inspector	63, 68
Medicaid swindler	63
Medicare	86, 90, 93
Medium is the Message, The	148
Meet the Press	111, 121
Menuhin, Yehudi	65
Miami, Florida	21, 89, 90
Mickel, Clay	98
minimum wage	41
Modern Health Care, magazine	85
Modern Hospital	85
Montgomery Ward	85
MTV	112
"Muppets, The"	80
National Enquirer	66, 114, 120
NBC	71, 114, 115, 117-120
New York Philharmonic	65
New York Times	80, 84, 145, 147, 154
New York, New York	2, 21, 31, 40, 47, 114
Newman, Edwin	22
NFL Football	115
Nielsen	118-120
Nightline	96, 121, 154
Nightly News	138
Nixon, President Richard	62, 63, 85
North Carolina	125
North Texas State University	141

Not Quite Ready for Prime Time 70, 112
nuclear power plants 51, 52
Nuclear Regulatory Commission 53
Nunn Committee 97-99
Nunn, Senator Sam 96, 99, 104, 105
Olian, Catherine 74
Olympic Games 85
Oprah 154
"Orange Juice Man, The" 79
ozone layer 41
Palmer, Marti Galovic 74
Panama 80
Parade magazine 69
Pauley, Jane 115
pentagon 77, 80
People magazine 63
Persian Gulf 80
polygraph 5, 12-14, 17
President of the United States 123, 125
Prime Time Live 61, 70, 77, 112-114, 117,
                                                    119, 137-139, 154
Puerto Rico 128
Quayle, Dan 15
Queeg, Captain 12
Radio/Television News Directors Association 20
Rather, Dan 55, 59, 62, 63, 66-68,
                                                    80, 114, 115
Reagan, Ron 116
Reagan, Ronald 136
Reagan-era 44
Reasoner, Harry 24, 29, 31-37, 51-53, 55, 62-64, 66,
                                        68-71, 74, 78, 84, 85, 87-91, 93, 94
Republican 96, 126
Rhode Island 30, 32, 34
Rich, Frank 80
Richard, Shirley 1-3, 5, 6, 8-10, 14, 17
Rocky Mountain News 50
Rogers, Les 29, 31
Rooney, Andy 24, 62, 68
Rosenberg, Howard 98-100, 102, 103, 118, 119
Rotary Clubs 54
Rummel, David 78
Safer, Morley 24, 62, 63, 65, 68-70, 72, 74, 80
salmonella poisoning 123, 124
San Diego Federal Savings and Loan Association 58

San Diego, California 58
San Francisco, California 10
Sawyer, Diane 61-63, 67, 68, 70, 112-114, 123
Schaffer, Archie 126, 128, 129
Scottsdale Princess Hotel 102, 103, 107, 108, 110
Secretary of Agriculture 132
Senate, U.S. 95
Sickler, David 12, 14
Siegel, Alan 139
Simpsons, The 119
60 Minutes Minute by Minute 62
South American beef 41
Springdale, Arkansas 124, 126, 128, 130
Stahl, Leslie 22, 23, 25, 42, 62-64,
                                            66, 67, 74, 98-109
State Department 22
Stossel, John 112
"Stradivari" 80
Street Stories 96, 114, 115
styrofoam 41
Switzerland 118
tabloids 120
Talking Back to the Media 15, 59
Tax Code, U.S. 101, 105
"Teddy Kollek of Jerusalem" 80
Texas Insurance Commissioner 105
"This House is a Steal" 127
This Week with David Brinkley 138, 139
Thompson, Charles C., II 76, 77, 80
Thompson, J. Walter 2, 31
Tiffin, John 74, 80
Time 120
tobacco industry 116
tobacco lobby 42
Today Show 115, 154
Tollett, Leland 126
Tresnowski, Bernard 85-94, 96, 98-109
20/20 .... 43, 61, 77, 112, 114, 117,
                                      119, 137, 138, 145, 154
Tylenol murders 141, 143, 144, 155
Tyson Foods 64, 123-133, 135
Tyson, Don 125-135, 154
United Press International 20, 31
University of North Texas 141

163

USA Today 138, 139
"USS Iowa" 80
"Victims of Just Cause" 80
Vieira, Meredith 62, 63, 67-69, 74
Wall Street Journal 52, 54, 83, 84, 86, 154
Wallace, Mike . . . . v, xi, xii, 1-15, 17, 19, 21-25, 28, 33, 45, 46,
                            58, 62-66, 68-70, 72-74, 128-135, 138, 139
Walmart 126
Walters, Barbara 9, 61, 63, 112, 114
Walton, Sam 126
Warrenville, Illinois 84
Washington Post 84
Washington, D. C. 40, 43, 44, 67, 77, 85,
                                              97, 98, 114, 126, 132
Wasserman 42
Watergate 52, 138
West Virginia 95, 96
Whipple, Chris 78
White House 21, 63, 67, 98, 130
Whitewater 126
Wortham, Bob 57
You Are the Message 15, 148
Zenker, Arnold 22

TO ORDER ADDITIONAL COPIES

Please send me _____ copies of

"Sunday Showdowns with **60 Minutes**"

at $9.95 per copy.

(Shipping and handling charges will be paid by the publisher.)

Check enclosed _____   Please bill me _____

Ship to: _____
(Name   Please Print)

_____
(Street Address)

_____
(City,   State,   Zip Code)

_____
(Signature)

Send order to:
    Arena Publishing Co.
    Business Book Div.
    Box 174
    660 Preston Forest Cntr
    Dallas, TX 7530-2718

Ken Fairchild is president of Fairchild/Oppel, a division of Publicis Public Relations, specializing in media training and crisis consulting. Based in Dallas, the firm operates worldwide. After a career in radio and television news in New York, Houston, and Dallas, Fairchild became one of the originators of "spokesperson" training in 1973.